# THE REAL MACKAY

# THE REAL MACKAY

Being Essays by Ian Mackay

*Edited by Stanley Baron*
*With Illustrations by Vicky*
*and a Profile by R. J. Cruikshank*

*London,* 1953
"NEWS CHRONICLE" PUBLICATIONS DEPARTMENT
12/22, BOUVERIE STREET, E.C.4

*Printed in Great Britain by The Hollen Street Press Limited, London, W.1*
*and published by the*
*" NEWS CHRONICLE" PUBLICATIONS DEPARTMENT*
*12/22, Bouverie Street, London, E.C.4.*

# CONTENTS

v

# CONTENTS

# PROFILE by R. J. Cruikshank

IAN MACKAY was born John Mackay at Wick in 1898. He was re-born Ian only when he joined the *News Chronicle* thirty-six years later. Various reasons have been put forward to explain re-christening, as indeed there are various theories about almost everything concerning the life and nomenclature of this remarkable character. It is enough to say that "Ian" is the Gaelicism of "John". And it is as Ian Mackay that the wide circle of his friends and readers will always recall him.

He went to Wick High School, and left it—with a legendary reputation for scholarship—at the age of fourteen.

On that slender basis of formal education he built, with the aid of his mother, the wide, luminous and humane structure of knowledge familiar to all who knew him.

The maternal Mackay was an astonishing woman who brought up her three sons, of whom Ian was the eldest, by her own efforts. All her spare pence, earned by domestic work, were spent on books—good books, classics, the best of the world's literature. Her sons, the eldest especially, swallowed them whole. When she moved in 1927 from her cottage in the shadows of "the biggest kippering kiln on earth" this hard-won library included over 3,000 volumes.

Ian's own contribution to it had been characteristically earned by personal sweat. For 2d. a time while still at school he rose at six in the morning to hump coal for his mother's neighbours; at night he worked a two or three hour newspaper round.

Cricket claimed him as a devotee, but Wick knew him as a strong outside-right who, some elderly local experts think, could have made his name in professional football.

He spent three years in the pharmacy of W. Gow Miller, a great influence in his life, and as I write, in the little heap of papers before me on the table is a certificate from the chemist dated 14th October, 1915, "That John Mackay has been engaged for all the last three years in dispensing medicines in this establishment."

That, I imagine, was the certificate he took with him when he volunteered for the Army. He was seventeen then, at least a year under the official age. Not even his mother, waving goodbye to a trainful of volunteers steaming away from Wick station, knew her son was among them. He served for four years in the Royal Army Medical Corps, being attached for a long period to the Irish Rifles. In the selections from Ian Mackay's work which he has made for this book, Stanley Baron has included the charming piece on "Wick Revisited" which he wrote in 1938. This reveals the heart and inspiration of much of his later writing.

Stanley Baron writes to me, "Here are the kippering sheds, the Bleaching Green, South Road and the Town Hall which cropped up over and over again in those allusive introductions to so many wildly assorted subjects. Not to mention Grandmother Hughina who 'had such a high opinion of the Devil—whom she called Sahtan—that she wouldn't even strike a match on a Sabbath' and used to give Ian a 'skelping' every morning on the principle that 'I would surely have earned it by night'; his mother, well known to Wick as an anti-clericalist; his Aunt Magersfontein; his father Angus Mackay the engine driver who once sneezed his false teeth straight from the footplate into Lough Shin, and died of a strange encounter with a haystack; the apothecary, his first regular employer, who 'lived on peaches and chianti'; and all the rest of the glorious gallimaufry to whom Ian traced back most of the later events of his life. Around them he wove his legends with an inventiveness and abandon certainly never excelled in Greece.

"What struck me most, while re-reading the million words or so he wrote for the *News Chronicle* during his last seven years, has been not merely the staggering range of his interest and the intensity of his curiosity, but the sense of fantasy behind it all.

"This was peculiar and personal. Everything in his life, that would be humdrum in ours, was touched with richness and strangeness. When I first met him he was a lean, incredibly dishevelled giant, with (as another friend described it) 'the North wind for hair' and a wife, Loma, who was sawn in half twice nightly by his father-in-law.

"Devoted women tidied him up but never cured the fantasy. There was the night he wilfully set fire to his hair—which didn't change its colour much, it being already a kind of charred crimson, but certainly cleared The Cogers bar, where it happened. And the night he ate the daffodils.

"With new acquaintances he had an enormous and kindly gift for discovering at once what interested them and then bringing forth some appropriate anecdote—sometimes true, often invented, but always designed to please.

"To use a form of phrasing Ian himself was fond of—not since Rudolph Erich Raspe wrote the Travels of Baron Munchausen has a writer so plausibly and engagingly enlarged on life.

"I don't know whether he ever worked a bare-foot passage to Norway, but he declares he did, while at the same time insisting, 'It's not the truth which matters so much as the feeling behind the truth.'

"I am sure his confession was true that 'to this day, wherever I am, I turn over a kipper box to see if it comes from Wick, as Arnold Bennett used to turn up plates and saucers to see if they were from Stoke; and Delius, no doubt, looked at the tabs on his combinations to see if they came from Bradford.'"

During the 1914 war Mackay made his first contributions to journalism by sending sketches from the trenches to the *John O'Groat Journal* and later the *Northern Ensign*. Sometime in the early twenties he came to London and took an ex-Serviceman's course at London University. During this period he is said to have kept himself afloat by writing sermons for ministers at two guineas each. One longs to know—were they all Presbyterian sermons? Among his other qualities he had a flavour of the Covenanter, and could argue predestination and original sin with the sternest of theologians. As Henley said of Stevenson, Mackay had in him "a deal of Ariel, just a streak of Puck and something of the Shorter Catechist."

Some of all these qualities found their way into the contributions, signed "Mac's Letters from a London Attic" (almost the forerunner of his famous *News Chronicle* Diary) which he continued to send to the *John O'Groat Journal*. He later on found a post on the *Piano Maker*, published in London by Herbert Sinclair, a fellow citizen of Wick. His entry into the wider world of journalism came with his appointment to the London staff of the *Western Morning News*. He came to know the House of Commons very well during this period. Variously he gave his first London address as Store Street and Howland Street, both of them off the Tottenham Court Road.

Mackay joined the *News Chronicle* as its industrial correspondent in 1934. Like all first-class journalists, he was at base a good reporter. He could take long verbatim stretches of speeches. Although he knew no shorthand, he once "filled in" for a *Daily Express* colleague who was in difficulties deciphering his own shorthand notes of Lord Beaverbrook.

In a world where accurate reporting and fair comment can affect the labour relations of a whole industry, his thoroughness and responsibility quickly won for him the trust of the entire trade union movement. His magnetic personality became as notable at the Trades Union Congress or the Labour Party Conference as any of the platform figures, and it was commonly supposed that he had achieved his final vocation. There was no one to prophesy then that the best newspaper diarist and essayist of our time was buttoned up inside the man who was so knowledgeable about trade union practice and labour relations.

It was Ian Mackay himself who discovered the dormant diarist. A somewhat startled editor received these first "intimations of immortality" from his industrial correspondent in the form of a commentary, published daily, on the events of the 1945 General Election. Such confines, it was evident, were far too narrow. It says a great deal for the discerning imagination of Sir Gerald Barry as an editor that he encouraged the fresh departure—as a general diary— at a time when newspapers were still in the iron bands of four pages and the tendency of editors was to chill the ardour of their staffs for writing at all.

The new feature at once attracted attention. It presented a fresh voice in journalism. It expressed a vibrant personality, warm-hearted, generous, with infectious gusto and an immense range of sympathies. In this book will be found a sampling of the Diary, the emergence of the essay, and the grand personality that was mirrored in both forms.

The manner of Ian Mackay's death on Friday, October 3rd, 1952, at the end of the Labour Party Conference at Morecambe, was sudden, shattering to his friends, yet surely as he would have wished. He had never seemed in fuller vigour, and just before he was struck down he had made the final speech of the Conference—the reply to the traditional vote of thanks to the Press, which he always did so well. On this occasion he was more gay and witty than ever before, and united in genial laughter an audience of three thousand that had been engaged in bitter dispute.

At the full height of his manhood, suffering as yet none of the sorrows or disillusions of his later years, he had indeed achieved a richness of maturity that glowed in all he did. Beside him, and very much part of him in this last phase, was his wife, the former Miss

Rosemary Say, whom he had married eighteen months previously. That so happy and fruitful a partnership should be so soon ended was the most cruel aspect of his death.

I am sure that no newspaperman has ever been so widely mourned. What struck me in the days after he died was the stream of letters that poured in from all parts of the country, in which men and women who had never seen him in their lives wrote as though they had lost their best friend. He had a unique power of attracting people's affections, and his generous personality expressed itself as effectively through the written word as the spoken. Somerset Maugham says somewhere that the great secret of writing is to convey the sound of the human voice. That most certainly was Ian's gift. He could illuminate his phrases with the warmth of his smile. There are some writers who, when they sit down to pencil and paper, appear to assume a kind of mandarin English which is quite distinct from their normal style of saying what they think and feel. Ian's writings were an extension of his personality, they reproduced the flavour of his talk.

Mackay had a rare power of communicating his personal magic to his readers. His heart was big enough to draw them all into the circle of his friendship. He could convey to them with swift directness the experience that had made him happy, or that had sent him into a blaze of wrath. He was the good companion of numberless men and women who had never set eyes upon him. It was this gift of conveying the electrical discharges of his spirit that made him the most successful personal columnist of his day.

The camera seldom did him justice. In a photograph that striking head of his with its revolutionary shock of hair, might resemble that of a pioneer of European Socialism, a friend of Jean Jaurés or Liebknecht. In real life it was likely to be thrown back in delighted appreciation of some flashing phrase or a piece of comic invention.

He once described his face to me as being the craggiest and rockiest ever to come out of Scotland. It was, in truth, the friendliest.

His friendships were catholic and enthusiastic. They ranged from Pierrepoint the Hangman to Ministers of State. Mere listeners were of no use to Ian. His closest friends were themselves great talkers. Once in order to continue a conversation with a fellow industrial correspondent whose duties were taking him to Wigan, Ian took the train to Wigan too.

Such friends have their own special categories of recollections.

There are those for whom he was above all the good companion of a hundred sorties into the taverns of the town. There were others, no less warm, to whom he was an unforgettable figure who had once passed by. Sometimes the two overlapped, as at the annual Children's Christmas Party at the Fitzroy Tavern, where Ian himself played Father Christmas, distributing chocolates sent specially for the occasion by such American devotees of the Mackay charm as Miss Shirley Temple.

His ailments (some real and painful) might cramp his stomach but never his style, either in writing or good fellowship. Thus, well known both to personal friends and readers, there was his "beaker of bismuth" period, duly documented in reports and essays dispatched from anywhere between Blackpool and the Balkans.

Fleet Street is a place which likes to know where its correspondents are. It would be truer, in Ian Mackay's case, to say that often his editor, like Ian himself, knew where he *had* been or where he was supposed to be, only by reading the current morning's *News Chronicle*, containing his Diary or report with date-line.

"Away from home," he confided blandly, "the first thing I do is to send for the morning's newspapers, so that I can start the day at least knowing what town I'm in."

The paper's reward was reporting of the highest level.

His zest for life was boundless. There were at least half a dozen men wrapped up in him. For example, there was the Mackay who was the passionate book-lover. He has told me that every day of his life since he was a boy he had read a page from Shakespeare. He had a vast knowledge, not only of the classics, but of the strangest by-ways of literature.

He could easily have devoted his life to libraries and literary criticism, but his warm sympathies, his curiosity about human beings which was like the measureless curiosity of a Dickens or Balzac, and his passion for justice drew him out into a far wider world than that of books. Going past St. Bartholomew's Hospital early one morning he took the brush from an old woman scrubbing the steps and finished the job himself.

There was the Mackay who had a fantastic knowledge of the music-hall songs of times past. The death of a veteran of variety would bring from him an enchanting essay which had the quality of Sickert's paintings of the Old Bedford.

Again, there was the Mackay who had an uncanny learning about old houses and inns and the visitations of historic figures.

Or one was suddenly caught up by the Mackay who was the connoisseur of the quiddities and eccentricities of men and women, the keeper of an Old Curiosity Shop of human nature. He rejoiced in rare facts as in odd folk. As Stanley Baron reminds me:—

"He turned over everything, even (or especially) such colourful publications as *The Board of Trade Journal*, from which he once discovered that 'while witches can come in free, under Import Control Order 292, broomsticks are still banned.'

" 'Ever since the day I discovered, quite by accident as I was doing a school sum, that the number 9 has magical properties not possessed by any other number, I have been fascinated by statistics,' he wrote.

" 'It doesn't seem like 26,729,280 minutes' was the heading to a piece he did on his 50th birthday, a date incidentally he claimed to share with 'Shakespeare, Cervantes, Turner, Hardy, Anson, Allenby, Lord Haw-Haw, Cripps, Simone Simon, Charlie Brooks of the Manchester Press Club, Ethelred the Unready and Shirley Temple.' He was in fact born not on St. George's Day, but on April 24th. 'What sort of a man would I be,' he confessed, 'to let a mere 24 hours stand between me and Shakespeare?'

"An Electrical Communications list provided him with both a splendid piece about the horrors of telephones and the enchanting discovery that Hawaians, making 474 calls per head per year, are the most talkative people on earth.

"And why *did* Dickens spend £25 on whisky and rum in the second half of May, 1866?

"Ian's passion for London was the obverse of his escape from Wick.

" 'When you scratch a Scot you find a Cockney,' and for this Scot there was no smell, town or country, like 'the asphalt burners in the Strand.' "

His little idiosyncrasies were endearing. With any writing to which he attached especial importance—his Saturday essays, for example— he could not work without his pet fountain pen, once going to the trouble of travelling all the way from his home at Hampstead to the office to recover it. "I am pernickety, too," he declared, "about my ink. It must be blue, the lighter blue the better, and even then I can only write on white paper."

When you talked to him he seemed timeless. He summed up in

himself generations of Fleet Street. He was the inheritor of the great tradition of the essayist-journalist which was begun by Leigh Hunt and Hazlitt and came down to Mackay in direct line of descent through G. K. Chesterton and Robert Lynd.

He was overflowing with images, memories, comic notions, scraps of poetry and an encyclopaedia of allusions. He was a scholar who knew the life of mean streets and trade union lodges. He was at one and the same time an authority on Dr. Johnson and Marie Lloyd, on Keir Hardie, Sherlock Holmes and the Dixie Kid. He could evoke with equal grace the Wick of his boyhood and the Old Provence of legend. He was, above all, the happy humanist, a man who believed in the power of laughter to wither evil and protect the good.

He would never agree that to be a reformer a man must be sour, or that solemnity is the badge of virtue, or bile a sign of grace. He was a Radical in the Dickens tradition. He was an optimist in the Chesterton tradition.

That means he liked the human race. He never sought to regiment or improve men and women for their own good. He wanted to see them freed from tyrannies and abuses in order that they might choose their own happiness in their own way. He had a romantic faith in the restoration of Merrie England—and in late years he made many converts to that cause.

Ian Mackay was essentially one of those men who are bringers of happiness. He was moving steadily from being the diarist of daily events to the essayist who ranges through a wider ether. His finest qualities were developing in this medium, and one has the melancholy sense that his best achievements were still to come.

Mackay could attack some wrong, some mean injustice, some petty hypocrisy with the muscular vigour of William Cobbett, and when his heart was touched he could write with that tenderness and grace which only the really masculine writers achieve.

His sympathies were constantly widening. His absorption in the human comedy had an all-embracing charity.

Ian's personality glows like a warm fire on a winter evening as we remember him. We hope that this book will bring pleasure to all his readers—which means all his friends. It is representative of his wonderful variety of moods and breadth of sympathies and so has something for everyone.

# PART ONE

# Talking of Wick

## THE PLACE WHERE I WAS BORN

### WICK.

IT was strange to come back to Wick on a bleak winter morning straight from the gay and glittering boulevards of Paris and Brussels. Save for two fleeting visits several years ago it was exactly 23 years since Lord Kitchener found me drudging away in a druggist shop and lured me to Flanders to lay the foundations of Fascism and make the world dangerous for democracy. Since then, like Ulysses, I have seen many men and cities and at times I regret to admit I have almost forgotten the old grey town where I was born forty years ago. It was good for me therefore to come back and it was particularly pleasing to return as I left in a blinding snowstorm and had to fight my way across the Bridge against a whistling wind which the driving snowflakes seemed to make solid and visible.

My first impression was of the "lowness" of the place. Buildings which used to tower to the stars when I was a boy seemed to have shrunk into shacks, and I felt I wanted to give the Town Hall an affectionate pat on the dome as I went by. I felt rather like Gulliver in Lilliput for an hour or so until I regained my sense of proportion. For some reason I remembered the reply which one of the Wick "worthies" once gave to a somewhat arrogant Londoner. "I suppose," said the Cockney, "that when the Highland line is snowed up you may be cut off for a whole week and not know what is going on in London?" "Aye," replied the old man, "that happens now and then. But then ye see the people in London are no' better off. For a whole week they don't know what's going on in Wick."

Robert Louis Stevenson, who lived in Wick for a year when his father was trying in vain to build a breakwater—the ruins of which you can still see at low-water off the cruel rocks of Shaltigoe—described it as "the meanest of men's towns on the baldest of God's bays." I suppose it must have been a pretty miserable place for a consumptive away back in 1868; indeed, even in my boyhood days it was a dreadful place in the wintertime. There was no electric light. In most of the houses there wasn't even gas and I never saw a bathroom until I left the Army in 1919. This was not because of poverty—though God knows we were poor enough—for my well-to-do playmates were no better off.

Today things are different. The streets are well-lit, electric light and power are laid on in many of the houses, and altogether there is a more civilized look about the place. At the same time as I walked along the riverside in the twilight I felt sorry to think that never again shall I meet Leerie, the lamplighter—that municipal Prometheus —with his long pole. We used to regard him as a magician and run round the town with him on windy nights hoping that his mysterious light would blow out so that we could laugh at him striking matches in the wind and the rain. When the town was flooded—and this happened nearly every year in the lower district beside the river—Leerie went his round in a boat like a Venetian linkman in Casanova's time. That is about as far as we had got in Wick when the madman in Serajevo threw the bomb that blew us all up and scattered us to the four winds of Heaven. I often wonder what would have happened to us all but for the war. Perhaps I would now be punching pills with a mortar and pestle and selling lipstick to supercilious young ladies. Or I might have gone to sea as so many of my generation did.

The sea was the open road of escape for those who longed for a wider and fuller life. This all came back to me as I stood on the Station cliff above the river beside the cannon—a relic of some old war or other— and looked along the railway lines. I remembered so clearly how I used to watch the trains go off carrying my more fortunate schoolmates away into the world of romance and adventure, away to the shining cities and the great industrial centres of the South, which sometimes pushed out a fascinating feeler in our direction in the shape of a returned traveller. Usually we regarded these lucky devils who had escaped as "swanks" and we did not always believe the tremendous tales they told of their conquests in Edinburgh and London. But they always had money in their pockets, their clothes were smarter, their voices had altered and their obvious delight when their visit came to an end and they set off again over the mountains made a deep impression on the more imaginative of us.

After such a traveller had been in town I always felt restless. I would walk the streets as usual with my friends discussing the eternal verities as if nothing had happened, but inside I would rage and fume. There was I, a melancholy moon circling round and round in a monotonous orbit—making zinc ointment and linseed poultices—when I wanted to be a flaming comet rushing away into the infinite. It took me years to learn that comets, too, have their prescribed orbits and come back at last as regularly as the moon.

But youth in Wick was not all longing and frustration. It was a grand place for boys. The sea, the rocks and the river, the Loch of Watten, the quiet pools near the Fairies' Hill, where we used to bathe naked, the islands and the rushing weirs, where we sometimes caught salmon with our hands, the wireless station, the Newtown burn which foamed like a river of stout in the flood season, the distillery, the refuse tip, the library, the harbour, Geddes's Yard, where they killed the geese at Christmas, the slaughter-house, the fish-curing yards, the auction mart and a hundred other places provided us with plenty of amusement. And in winter, when the great storms turned the bay into a raging fury, we loved to tempt the tempest and dash along the quay between the crashing waves. Once a year we would venture as far as Thurso—the sister town 20 miles away—and return late at night full of lemonade and mutton-pies, with the swagger of Vasco da Gama.

I suppose the boys of today do the same things. I cannot tell, for I saw very little of them. The town has declined in population and there seemed to be fewer children about. I found, too—as A. J. Cummings did in Barnstaple—that the invasion of the multiple shops has robbed the town of much of its old charm and individuality.

"Good morning, Mr. Davidson," I used to say when my mother sent me for a half a dozen eggs and a pound of cheese. "How is your mother getting on?" the old boy would answer and he would give me a handful of conversation lozenges or a stick of black sugar and tell me to give my mind to my home lessons. Today things have changed. How can you say "Good morning, Home and Colonial Stores" or "It's a fine day, Mr. Woolworth"? They wouldn't hear you if you did.

I spent a long time on the old "Bleaching Green" beside the river, for in the old days this was the dearest place of all. It was here that they held the Hill Market—Wick's annual fair—and here, too, it was that the circus and the travelling theatre would pitch their tents in the summer time. We knew when the circus was coming and some of us would get up at dawn and walk for miles along the South Road to meet the elephants and the camels. And when the week was over and

3

they went away, I would stand in the pale green withered circle where the ring had been and cry. We collected the glittering sequins which fell from the uniforms of the lovely ladies as they galloped round the ring, and I think my mother may have a box of them yet. The travelling theatre—the cinema has killed it now, I am told—was a canvas tent and we used to sneak in under the flaps with the watchman's whip lending speed and subtlety to our posteriors.

The harbour which was once the busiest herring port in the world is nearly dead now, and apart from a few foreign sailors and some unemployed men I had the place to myself and the screaming gulls. The greatest of all changes I have left to the last. In my youth Wick was one of the most drunken towns on the face of the earth. Today it is dry, and unless you are a member of one or two clubs you cannot get a drink, not even in your hotel. It is arguable as to whether the town has benefited from this great social and moral reform. It certainly keeps people away, and those who can afford it can either join the club or take the train to Thurso or Lybster, where the publicans are all in favour of prohibition as long as it is confined to Wick. There is, I was told, a special train to Thurso on Saturdays which a wag in Thurso described as "The Flying Distillery."

I met few of my boyhood friends, as most of my generation were either killed in the war or have wandered away to the ends of the earth. Probably I would meet more of them in Manitoba or Queensland. On the whole my visit was a sad business, and I don't think I shall ever go back again.

*February 10th*, 1938

## THE RIPPLE WAS RANJI

WHEN I was a lad up in Wick in the days of the Peacemaker when Sankey and Moody were singing their way to salvation, Jessop was hitting sixes over the steeple at Gloucester, Campbell-Bannerman was laying the foundations of the Commonwealth and Marie Lloyd still had a saucy little twinkle in her eye, there used to be in the auld grey toon a remarkable old rogue we all called "Johnny-likes-a-haddie." We called him that because he seemed to live almost exclusively on the scraps of sun-dried haddock that the fishwives flung to him in the narrow dark smoky and noisome hole in the wall that served him for a home.

He commenced his working life as a plumber, but after reading Thoreau he became a pantheist. But there is something about pantheism which does not mix with plumbing, and after a vain attempt to combine Thoreau and tapwater he gave it up, collected a few books, a bedstead and a paraffin lamp and retired forever to his malodorous hermitage.

As the years went by he grew dirtier and dirtier and wiser and wiser. His whiskers, which were sable when he entered his retreat, turned to silver and later on to snow, and in the end they covered all you could see of him except his merry, laughing eyes, which we could see dancing in the darkness when we looked into his den. Many praiseworthy efforts were made to "redeem" him and to clean the place up, but to all such reformers he gave the same answer that his master Diogenes gave to Alexander 23 centuries before: "Get out of my light." When he died, except for his tortoise, canary, his white mice and the books and the bedstead, they put all his possessions in a small paper bag and then they buried him in the pauper's corner of the cemetery among the tramps and the tinkers under a slab of freestone which told us his name was John Dunnett.

What, you may well ask, has brought this odd character back into my mind after all these years? Believe it or not, old Johnny was conjured up from the grave by a queer combination of Ranjitsinhji, Perrault's Fairy Tales and a Press cable from Washington about the love life of the sperm whale. First of all the cable, which came from Arthur Edson, the Associated Press man in Washington, says that in a report on whale life in the Antarctic a Dr. Raymond Gilmore has announced that some whales have a lot of love life while others have none at all. Quite a few whales are spurned altogether by the females and they go right away down to the Antarctic or up to the North Pole to sulk. These are usually the ones harpooned, as they don't care anyway, so remember when you get your teeth into that nice juicy whale steak that you are probably devouring all that remains of some poor lovelorn Romeo of the deep whose girl friend gave him the air.

This poignant tale set me thinking about "Moby Dick," and as I had lost my copy I went along to buy a second-hand one. I failed but came away with a priceless gem which cost me just five bob. It was Andrew Lang's cheap pasteboard edition of Perrault's Popular Tales.

A poor "buy," you would say! But on the flyleaf what do you think I found? The book plate of the great "Ranji" himself. It shows a lion rampant bearing a pennant with the words, "Nil Desperandum," and beneath that it says: "The Maharajah Jam Sahib of Nawanagar, Jamnagar." That was music enough you would have thought! But on the page opposite in ink, written by that famous hand by the very wrist that wrought such sweet magic on so many green fields when all the world was young, is inscribed: "H.H. Maharajah Jam Sahib, Staines." The date is July 27, 1908.

On that day, Wisden tells us, Ranji batted for six hours at the Oval and scored a double century. And then he went along to Sotherans, bought Perrault, and went home to Staines to read about Cinderella, the Sleeping Beauty and Puss in Boots! Which brings me back to "Johnny-likes-a-haddie" in his hideous hole. For he told me one night as I was bandaging his leg that everything everywhere at all times is linked directly up with everything else. "When a polar bear coughs at the North Pole," he said, "there is an infinitesimal ripple on the sands of the Sahara." It was Dr. Gilmore's researches into the activities of the cetaceous Casanovas of King Haakon's Land that made me search for Moby Dick and find Cinderella and Ranji. But what is more, before he retired to his lair, old Johnny was a great Ranji fan and to the end he used to follow the averages by the dim light of his smoky lamp. And when the Australians came to Wick in 1912 I asked Whitty and Frank Laver to come along to see him and he kept them laughing for an hour.

*July 15th, 1947*


## KOHEBRAHAMA DID MY TEETH

IT seems a far cry from the Market Place in Wick to the White House in Washington. And an even further one from President Truman to a roguish old coon called Kohebrahama who ruined my teeth when I was a lad of 12. But they came together yesterday when I received a message from one of Truman's "trusties" in the American capital. Before I come to that, however, I must tell you who this old rogue was. Though he has long been dead and gathered to his jungle gods he stands out in my mind as one of the major, and certainly one of the most colourful influences in my life.

Kohebrahama looked for all the world as if he had been created by the joint genius of Mark Twain, O. Henry and Al Jolson. He looked like a cross between Uncle Tom, Monolulu and a boot polish advertisement. His skull, which was smooth and shiny as a black billiard ball, was fringed with lambswool curls, and when he laughed his teeth glimmered like snowdrops in a crimson cave. He wore a shepherd tartan suit and a yellow waistcoat with mother-of-pearl buttons, patent leather shoes which answered the shine of his skull, green spats and a vermilion topper on which appeared the words "Whiter than snow" in silver letters.

At night he lit a lamp inside his hat—the first illuminated sign ever seen in Wick. To gather a crowd he played Negro melodies like "Swanee," "Camptown Races," and "Poor Old Joe," and when we crowded round his cart recited poems about Dixie and Tennessee which he said were written by Burns, Shakespeare, Milton and John Bunyan. Then when we were all in a jolly mood Kohebrahama put his hat and banjo aside, produced a mysterious wicker basket and asked for a lad to join him on his cart. That is where I came in and my teeth began to come out. For, I regret to report retrospectively, I became Kohebrahama's assistant for one whole summer. Need I tell you he was a quack dentist? Or that his basket was packed with magical new radio-active tooth powders which not only kept the teeth white and the breath pure, but aided digestion, staved off night starvation, cured heartburn and generally improved the system.

My job was to have my teeth covered with soot and then polished with the magic powder. Kohebrahama was kind, efficient and excitingly entertaining and every night he gave me 6d. and a tin of the powder, which was just chalk and fishbone. It did for my teeth in record time and for every 6d. I earned as Boy Friday I must have spent £6 putting them right.

This all came back to me when I read the report from Washington about the Quacks Chamber of Horrors run by the Food and Drug Administration. In the letter which accompanied it Truman's friend —a famous labour leader who also suffered under Kohebrahama— tells me that in spite of the Government's vigilance America is getting more quack-ridden every day. Only the other day a "Doctor" Ghadiali, of Bombay, was fined 20,000 dollars and sent to Sing Sing for three years for selling a gadget called the "spectrochrome," which he claimed would cure anything by coloured lights. Yellow and magenta "cured" diabetes, green cured syphilis and violet tuberculosis. A tartan beam, presumably, would cure everything.

My favourite phoney nostrum, however, is a device like a pencil, which costs only £150. Its modest inventor claims it will "absolutely cure bronchial trouble, toothache, sinus conditions, burns, injuries and *all illnesses in general.*" I like that final claim. It reminds me of the man at the Socialist conference who rushed to the rostrum, after somebody had proposed to nationalise all the means of production, distribution and exchange in United Europe, and moved to add the words, "and the solar system." Old Kohebrahama was never quite so Napoleonic as that, though he did recite some ribald rhymes about Josephine. He destroyed my teeth but I forgive it him. May his gods rest his soul wherever it may be among the ghostly jungle drums. I wonder who is strumming his banjo now!

*February 23rd,* 1950


## WHAT A MAN WAS MY FIRST BOSS!

WHEN I was throwing away some old calendars the other night, I came across an entry which reminded me that if he had not died suddenly during the first World War, my earliest employer would have been 90 years of age today. And as he was a very great influence in my life—he colours my mind even now—I hope you will bear with me while I pay a tribute to his memory, even if you call me a sentimental old josser for doing so. He was an interesting chap and through him you may get a glimpse of that strange vanished era which seems farther away from us now than the days of Good Queen Bess. For, as we all know, Shakespeare, Donne and Drake are much nearer to us in word and spirit than Pinero, Hall Caine and Lord Charles Beresford.

In the second decade of this tormented century, when I was a freckled urchin in a chemist's shop in Wick, my employer was the most remarkable man in the town. In fact, he was in many ways the most remarkable man I have ever met, although since then, like Ulysses, I have seen many men and cities. His name was William Gow Miller, and his rosy cheeks and friendly eyes shone with benevolence and good cheer. He wore queer coloured suits, fancy waistcoats, flowing ties with blue and white dots on them, romantic feathered hats with green and vermilion cords and ribbons and he always carried a yellow silver-headed cane which, with a flick of the wrist he could turn into a rapier.

There was a strange timeless look about him. As he strolled—for he could not be said to have walked—down the street he looked like one of the Cheeryble brothers dressed in Beau Brummel's fanciest suit. Every now and then he would emerge from the dispensary in green knickerbockers buttoned at the knees, which, with his corded hat and yellow stick, gave him the look of a Tirolean yodeller. On such occasions he brightened up and glorified the dull grey northern town.

He loved Chianti, smoked perfumed cigars, carried little muslin sachets of lavender in his pockets, took cocaine like Sherlock Holmes by the needle, and adored Mr. Asquith, whom he resembled when he was hatless among his jars and bottles. Though he died a bachelor he worshipped in a vague antiseptic sort of way a superb but disdainful siren who ran a hotel and wore feather boas all the year round. Nothing ever came of this, though she must have spent a fortune on sedatives and cosmetics making up to him. He lived with his sisters, two aged, arid but affectionate spinsters in a bleak house beside an even bleaker burn at the back of beyond.

For all that, his knowledge of the world, like Mr. Weller's knowledge of London, was extensive and peculiar. Unlike Mr. Weller's, it was expensive as well. For he lived a double life. From October to July he pounded away at his pills and powders and mixed his liniments and lotions in that queer *quant. suff.*, three-times-a-day-after-food world in which druggists live among their spirit lamps, sealing wax, orris root and alembics. But when summer came, he lived in a different world, on the Riviera, in the Engadine, in Madeira or the Costa Brava. Then he was the English milord in panama and white suit, a leisured sybarite dawdling from one luxurious resort to another, and living deliriously beyond his means. Early in August, when his annual supplies of castor oil and copaiba were safely delivered in big fat barrels, he went on to the Continent—he called it the *Conteenong*—leaving the shop in charge of a Welsh student, myself and an English lad who was afterwards devoured by a lioness in the Mountains of the Moon. He was away for two months, but every day we would get a glossy postcard from places like Bordighera and Seville. And now and then a packet of

9

snapshots would arrive showing him in a barouche on the Promenade des Anglais, on a camel in front of the Sphinx, in a gondola at Torcello, sipping a Pernod in the Cannebiere, standing on Vesuvius with a wisp of smoke behind him or knee-deep in the water at Viareggio with a cross to mark the spot where Shelley's body was burnt.

Then one day in October he would be back so brown that his teeth shone like snow and everybody would feel happier. He brought little odds and ends for all of us; bright coloured little things that brought a whiff of magic and romance into our icy little lives. For weeks he would potter about with his Chianti flasks and his new pictures, some of which were considered by the local bailies to be distinctly naughty. How he would have done today I cannot imagine. For he was a *fin de siècle* character and was lucky enough to live in his own good time. God bless him, wherever he is with his funny waistcoats and his crazy hats. How Sir Max would have adored him!

*January 12th*, 1952

## HOOPS, KITES AND HABAKKUK

WE have it on his own authority that Falstaff was once a boy, and that when he played truant from school he plucked geese and whipped his top. That was nearly six centuries ago, yet when I played truant only a few years ago I did exactly these things with an occasional raid on Sir Archibald Sinclair's waters when the salmon were running. I was never much of a goose plucker and whatever pleasure I got from poaching Sir Archibald's salmon was tempered by the Socialistic conviction that they were as much mine as his anyway. Incidentally, if I were a Tory I should condemn Socialism, not for its economic principles, which are sound, but on the ground that there is not nearly so much fun in stealing your own property as there is in robbing the boss.

Though I was not very good as a plucker of geese or as a poacher, as a whipper of tops and flier of kites I was unsurpassed north of the Grampians. At marbles, hopscotch and quoits I was never more than of third division calibre, and though I was a fairish hoop-trundler I could never keep up with a girl called Dulcie Alexander, who was fleeter of foot than Swinburne's "fleet-foot kid," and with whom I was deeply but dumbly in love. But my great top Habakkuk, which was as fat as an alderman, and shone like a rainbow at full spin, was the champion of the neighbourhood. And my home-made kite, which I called the Clipper of the Clouds, and painted to look like a mandarin with his pigtail streaming behind him, was the undisputed monarch of the northern skies. About this time of year when the English boys were oiling their bats and tightening up their rackets we used to wax our kites and polish our tops so that we should be ready for the March winds and smooth pavements when the snows were gone. That was not so very long ago and even after the first World War there were few boys—or girls for that matter—who did not have a hoop or a top.

Nowadays, so far as I can see, nobody ever whips a top or drives a hoop and, except in China and Constantinople, and among the grown-ups in Regent's Park, hardly anybody flies a kite. During the last fortnight I have been wandering about the lovely little towns and villages of Nottingham and Leicestershire and watching the youngsters at play. But though I have seen thousands of them romping about the roads and riversides, I have not seen one playing with a top, kite or hoop, or even skipping with a rope. The weather has been ideal for tops and hoops, if a little early for kites and sticky for marbles. Why is it that boys and girls don't play with tops and hoops any more?

Even in the school playgrounds where there is plenty of shouting and rushing about nobody plays at anything any longer. They just dash up and down, jump on parallel bars and slide down chutes without any apparent object except to let off steam. Never have so many expended so much energy doing so little. It may be that I am not so observant as I was, but it appears to me that children today do not play nearly so much with simple things as we used to do. They seem to have lost the art of enjoying themselves with a piece of wood, a bit of bent iron or a handful of marbles. It can hardly be the cost that stops them for we always made our own hoops, tops and kites. In fact, any boy who turned up with a shop top was usually whipped off the pavement.

My own view is that these simple, healthy, skilful and exciting games are being killed by the development of scientific and mechanical toys on the one hand and by the cinemas and municipal playgrounds on the other. One boy I asked about it the other day had never seen a hoop or a top and he gave up his kite when his uncle sent him an electric helicopter from America. Maybe I'm becoming an old fogy and the children of today get just as much fun out of their scientific gadgets as we got out of our home-made tops and kites. But I am sure they don't get nearly so much exercise and fresh air. Before long, no doubt, their children will be playing with atomic toys and having fun with fission and radar-controlled robots. And it may do them no harm. For all that, I can't help feeling it will be a bad day for the children when there are no hoops or tops spinning in the whole of England and the only kite-fliers left are the retired ironmongers and corn chandlers in Regent's Park.

*February 9th*, 1952

# PART TWO

# Aspects of Mackay

## HOSTILE SOCKS IN PICCADILLY

IT was recorded by one of the scandal-mongering columnists of the time that when the astronomer Halley called on his famous friend Newton at his rooms in Trinity one winter morning in Good King Charles's Golden Days he found the mathematical maestro in front of the fire gazing intently at an egg in his right hand while his watch—a brand-new silver and tortoise-shell turnip from Tompions —was boiling away merrily in the saucepan. That egg, I fancy, was produced by what the diplomatic correspondents call a "canard." But for all that it is a story that I feel sure the great army of absent-minded beggars would love to have been true.

It came back to me yesterday when Newton's watch began quite distinctly to tick in my mind right in the middle of Piccadilly Circus. Just as I was swinging myself on to a bus I suddenly noticed with a sickening shudder that I had come out among my fellow men wearing two socks of violently discordant colours. As I had just left the Cafe Royal, where they have a clock in the Marie Antoinette Room which works backwards, I thought for one wild moment that I was "seeing things," like Ray Milland in the film. But on closer inspection there was no doubt about it. My socks were not only different; they were definitely hostile! One was a drabbish grey, very quiet and peaceful, with a bluish cobwebby look about the heel, a nice gentlemanly sock that would be perfectly at home among the slumbering bishops in the Athenæum. The other—the left one, needless to say—was perfectly shocking. It was a really belligerent affair in the Buchanan tartan which —in case you don't know it—is the fiercest of all the barbaric garbs of old Gaul—a kind of a chromatic cross between Walt Disney's idea of the aurora borealis, sunset on the Yellow River and an explosion in a custard pie factory.

Why didn't I notice it when I put it on? I cannot say except that

I had to answer the 'phone—a wrong number—after I had put the quiet one on. The bold Buchanans I usually wear at week-ends to frighten the ducks in Regent's Park and I was sending them to the laundry in time to get them back before I go to climb the Matterhorn —the first hundred feet or so—at the end of the month. This was my first serious mental aberration since I left my teeth in one of Beaverbrook's tumblers in the "Night Scot" to Glasgow one night six years ago, when his lordship was turning saucepans into Spitfires. We were going up to the Clyde along with Davy Kirkwood to get the lads to put just one extra bit into it. They did, but I left my teeth in the train and I have never seen them since. Yesterday's faux pas, incidentally, revealed that I am not the man I was. Ten years ago I should have flourished my legs flamboyantly to show all the world what a mad fellow I was. Yesterday I slunk into a hosier's and spent five bob and a precious coupon on a pair of plain grey socks. Am I joining the bourgeois at last?

*August 3rd,* 1946


## IT HAPPENED ONE NIGHT

UNTIL I got home last night to find the lights all fused and the old ancestral halls plunged in dire and stubborn darkness, I imagined it was the ceaseless nagging and nattering of that hideous hag Xanthippe that made Socrates such a profound philosopher and dear old man. But after my desperate duel with the powers of darkness under my mansard roof in Marylebone I am now convinced that the old boy turned to metaphysics and high thinking after he had flattened that famous nose of his against one of the Parthenon pillars on his way home from a party one dark and sticky night.

After my frenzied gropings and stumblings midst a hellish legion of savage stools, sofas, buckets and boxes which slithered and snapped at my heels like clockwork crocodiles, as I floundered helplessly about looking for matches and candles, which were not there anyway, I am prepared to believe everything that Bacon, Edgar Allan Poe and Ambrose Bierce had to say about the dark. In the end I found my bed

—after skinning my shins on the iron frame—and slunk in between the sheets feeling about as civilised as a Neanderthal man wallowing down in his cave in the Dolomites ten million years ago.

But it did make me think about the slender hold we monarchs of all we survey really have on old Mother Nature. And one of the ponderous thoughts that kept coming up was that 99 per cent. of the miseries of mankind consist of the breakdown of artificial gadgets we have made ourselves in the last hundred years or so—lights fusing, cars breaking down, steamships sinking, trains crashing, phones going wrong, radio sets going dead, lifts not working, cigarettes running short, and so on. It makes you wonder whether all the scientific effort was really worth it, and emphasises the wisdom of old Thoreau, who maintained that happiness increases in direct proportion to the number of things you can do without. As for myself I have often wondered about the wisdom of a civilisation which discovered a method of getting from London to Widnes in four hours without first finding out if the place was worth going to at all.

*November 15th*, 1946

# MY GREATEST MOMENTS

YESTERDAY afternoon as I lay among the loosestrife and ragwort in the sparrow-haunted shadows of the Temple Library ruins, trying to concentrate on the Dungeon Scene in "Faust," I suddenly found my mind wandering in the queerest way to Rita Hayworth and the Lyric, Hammersmith. The air was busy with butterflies, the lawns were glowing with gaily-coloured girls, and even the hatchet-faced Chancery lawyers smiled like cold chisels as they watched the seed balloons of the willow herb sailing in silver over the shattered roof of Middle Temple Hall, where Elizabeth smiled on Shakespeare on the first night of "Twelfth Night."

I had just reached that tempestuous passage, in Bayard Taylor's translation, where Margaret flings her fetters down and cries to Faust —just before the Devil takes him—"Be quick. Be quick. Save thy perishing child," when my ears got the better of my eyes and I found

15

myself listening to a lass telling of her adventures in Hammersmith the other night. "We went to the Lyric," she said, "and they gave me the very seat Rita sat in the night before. I was thrilled." The dear thing fairly glowed with the wonder of it all.

It's queer how contact with the famous affects us all. In my job you would think I would have worked all that nonsense out of my system years ago. Prime Ministers, industrial caliphs and trade union rajahs leave me cold, but I still cannot resist a famous clown, artist, film star, murderer, centre-forward or fast bowler. Why, only a year or two before the war I nearly paid double for a bedroom at the Black Boy, Nottingham, when they told me that Don Bradman was the last man in. Then, shall I ever forget that morning in 1940 when I signed in at the Hotel Raphael in Paris, a day or two before Rundstedt took the place over, and the chambermaid told me, as she patted the pillows, that only two hours earlier they had been pressed by the lovely head of little Lily Pons, the world-famous warbler? And there was that great day in Whitehall Place when I hailed a cab and when it stopped, Bernard Shaw stepped out and I stepped in.

Then there was that magic night at Paganis in Great Portland Street, when I got the table just vacated by Puccini and Busoni, who left musical scribblings on the tablecloth among the wine stains and the breadcrumbs. Chesterton I frequently followed, of all places on earth, in a dairy tea shop in the Charing Cross Road, and once I found myself sitting next to Belloc on the top of a Chelsea bus. I can never make up my mind whether my biggest break was when Jack Dempsey mistook me for Carl Brisson in the Savoy Grill, when Horatio Bottomley knocked me down in Long Acre and offered me a five-pound note or the night when I found Charlie Chaplin sitting in my seat in the Press Gallery listening to Baldwin telling us our frontier was on the Rhine.

Best of all such stories, however, was told me during the war by old man Collinson, the Fleet Street taximan, who drove his cab through the blitz until he was nearly 90. One night in 1881 he picked up Lefroy, the Brighton train murderer, at Charing Cross just after he had done the deed, and drove him to Ludgate Circus. When he got out an old man like an eagle got in and cried: "House of Commons." It was Gladstone.

*July 29th*, 1947

## MY LONELY FURROW

ALTHOUGH it will be exactly three years tomorrow—at 8.35 p.m. precisely—since I went on the water wagon, very much as Sydney Carton mounted the guillotine, I woke up yesterday morning after a tempestuous night of turning and tossing with what you might call the Homer of all hangovers. My tongue was clean enough, my head was free from the old familiar fumes, and my heart was jogging along loyally at the regulation Harley Street rate. But in spite of all that, my eyes were bloodshot, my limbs weary and my loins aching, and I felt generally as one of the Dorias must have done after breakfasting with the Borgias. And, would you believe it, it was all the fault of Gray's Elegy!

Hitherto I have regarded that placid poem with its solemn owl, its yew-tree shade and drowsy tinklings in the distant folds, as the loveliest soporific in the language, sleepy and still as the grave. From now on, however, it is banished from my bedside. Henceforth it shall be read by me only on the tops of tramcars, at football matches and on the Great Racer at Blackpool. I shall never be able to sleep with it again. For when I reached it in the "Treasury" the other night I found myself playing games with the famous line about the ploughman plodding home.

Now, as even the Third Programme people know, Gray wrote: "The ploughman homeward plods his weary way," and that seems as good a way of putting it as any. Unfortunately, however, the imp who inhabits my brain, suddenly reminded me that it took Gray 30 years to write that line in that order and that my deskmate Ronald Walker —the man with the jet-propelled mind—claims to be able to write it 40 different ways. And so the night was ruined for me.

At three a.m. I was babbling "Homeward the ploughman plods his weary way," and at five I was muttering into my pillow "Weary the ploughman plods his homeward way." I tried all the tricks. At one o'clock I made tea, at two I took aspirin, at four I tried dialling TIM, and just as "the breezy call of incense-breathing morn" came wafting up from Barking Creek I gave myself a stiff shot of bismuth. But all was of no avail. That blasted ploughman kept plodding along. And just when I thought he had performed every evolution possible in seven words he broke into prose—a kind of Meredithian lope. "Homeward weary his way the ploughman plods." By the time the post came

17

he was plodding "his weary way homeward." The eight-o'clock News stopped him for about five minutes, but he paid no attention to the "Old Time Tunes" or the "Music For All" boys. As soon as Ramadier and Cripps were out of the way he was back on the road once more, this time to "plod weary homeward his way." After that there was no holding him. He took complete possession of the place, plodding here, there and everywhere.

All through this weary night it was small solace to recall every now and then that all the time in the narrow, comfortable cells the rude forefathers of the hamlet were sleeping away while this preposterous ploughman kept plodding around the room. Tonight I shall roll back the carpet and let him have his head, and place a litre of laudanum beside the bed instead of bismuth.

*October 24th,* 1947


# A WHIFF OF WHALEBONE

HOW many of you, I wonder, listened to that remarkable broadcast by Lady Violet Bonham Carter on Tuesday evening in which she described so entertainingly—and perhaps a little nostalgically— what it felt like to be a social butterfly during the opulent but precarious decade between the death of Victoria and the coronation of George the Fifth. It was such a wise, witty and perfectly phrased piece of sly social criticism that for a moment or two I fancied the whole thing was just another hoax and that it was Max Beerbohm himself doing a bit of female impersonation.

As I listened to Lady Violet's list of the conventions she had to observe after she "came out" I thanked goodness I was born in a Scottish slum and not in a Mayfair mansion. What a fussy little hell of do's and don'ts life must have been for a spirited young girl in those days, half-strangled with social taboos and fashionable fetishes like Laocoön struggling with the serpents. Lady Violet, being as brilliant as she was beautiful, managed to survive this ordeal, but it was interesting to hear that her famous step-mother, Margot Asquith, who was probably the most advanced woman of her time, warned her that she would commit social suicide if she was seen alone in a hansom with a young man. Incidentally, how Dickens would have loved Lady

Violet's description of the old "growler." It smelt, she said, of old straw and buttons.

It is largely owing to enlightened women like Lady Violet herself that life is more lenient on the young society girl of today. In fact, so far as freedom is concerned the maidens of Mayfair have nearly caught up with the dairymaids and fisher lasses of my young days, who contrived somehow to get by without the aid of chaperons.

Perhaps the most horrifying feature of this fascinating talk was Lady Violet's description of the hideous cages of steel and whalebone in which the poor Edwardian nymph was permanently encased. And many listeners must have been surprised to hear her call her blouse a "blooze." This was a real whiff from the whalebone days.

It reminded me of a horrid moment on my first night out in London when I called a vase a "vayze." "How quaint," said my hostess, who was the reigning dragon of Belgravia at the time. "I suppose you mean a vawze." This rankled for years, until one night during the blitz, when I found myself sitting next to John Winant at the Savoy. The Ambassador had been rambling among the ruins all day and he suddenly said: "I am quite sure now that Hitler can't win."

"What makes you say that," I asked. "Well," he replied in that slow, shy, shambling way of his, as an ack-ack gun barked on the Embankment, "it's like this. In Islington today I came across a woman in the ruins of her poor home and she was arranging a few sprays of lilac in a broken vayze, which she filled from a fireman's hose. What chance has Hitler got against her?"

My heart leapt for joy when he said vayze, and I looked back through the years and cocked a secret snook at that long-dead dragon who had so cruelly scorched my sensitive soul when I was a callow boy.

*March 5th,* 1948


## IT DOESN'T SEEM LIKE 26,729,280 MINUTES

ONE of the fondest illusions of my youth was the feeling that I would never grow old. It was an illusion shared by all my generation, and it is a fancy that will last as long as youth itself endures on earth. All the evidence was against us, from the white wind-bitten tombstones in the auld kirkyard to the old paupers who creaked like skeletons about the town. But what did that matter to immortal imps like us as we went skelping up the glens in the teeth of the winter wind, or spent whole summer days tumbling like salmon in the foam of the rushing weirs?

For when we are in our golden prime we are all like Cleopatra—age cannot wither us—and, as the hot blood bounds, we feel that Shakespeare's threat that golden lads and lasses must like chimney sweepers, come to dust, is just a bit of the Bard's immortal blarney. Some rare spirits—Ben Tillett and Ninon de L'Enclos are of the company—never lose the illusion and die as young as they were born. But for most of us the fancy cannot cheat for long. The cormorant years gobble us up and the dear delusion dies. The asp accomplishes what age cannot do to Cleopatra, the Flying Dutchman reaches port at last, and the golden girls, one by one, join Pocahontas in "the cool tombs." Even Peter Pan grows thin on top in time.

All this means that today is my 50th birthday. It is a solemn thought. Since that late Victorian morning when I arrived in Wick in the middle of a gowk storm I have managed to keep crawling on the crust of this ball of mud for 18,562 days and nights or, what is more astonishing still, 445,488 hours. It doesn't seem 26,729,280 minutes since I began and it's hard to believe my old heart has tick-tocked a thousand million times so far. But there it is and here I am. Being a Scot I arrived on St. George's Day just to be awkward. And I share the day with a very queer crew including Shakespeare, Cervantes, Turner, Hardy, Anson, Allenby, Lord Haw-Haw, Cripps, Simone Simon, Charlie Brooks, of the Manchester Press Club, Ethelred II, "The Unready" and Shirley Temple. And to show that Lord Woolton's system shares out the awards properly Shirley made more money before she was ten than all the rest of us put together in all our lives.

Well, I've lived through the second half of Mr. Cruikshank's "roaring century," and if you ask what I did during that time I will give you the answer Sieyès gave to a similar question at the end of the French revolution—"I survived." In the way of wear and tear I have lasted fairly well, though I cannot say, like old Adam in "As You Like It," that "in my youth I never did apply hot and rebellious liquors in my blood." Summing it up, I'd say the most tragic thing about my half century is that the uranium atom, which began it as a blessing, ended it as a menace to mankind. And the most hopeful thing is that the young immortals are still tumbling in the foaming weirs. For as our own immortal G. B. S. makes Cæsar say to Rufio, we may grow old and die but "the crowd upon the Appian Way is always the same age." Now for 1998!

*April 23rd, 1948*


## ALL MY EYE AND YVONNE DE CARLO . . . .

WHEN the Harley Street man told me three days before Christmas that I must have an operation on my eye and that he proposed—with the co-operation of Nye Bevan and myself—to do it on New Year's Day, the last thing I thought was that it would be so amusing. On the contrary, when I left his cosy Victorian salon— Gladstone used to live next door—I was fairly petrified with fear. For a moment or two I seriously considered going back by way of Hyde Park and joining Shelley's first wife Harriet at the bottom of the Serpentine. Then I heard a barrel organ a long way off playing "Beautiful Ohio" and I cheered up no end. And, believing with my fellow Highlander Macbeth that time and the hour runs through the roughest day, I turned my back on the Serpentine and went into the Mason's Arms—where Boswell and Weber had a dram in their day— and had a pint with Wilfred Pickles instead.

For the next 10 days I hugged my grisly secret to my bosom and applied myself to the walnuts and wine with the best of them. I even made a speech on the wireless about Joanna Baillie, who died a hundred years ago, forty years after Scott, on one of his daft days, said she was better than Shakespeare. And I danced a reel in the snow in Hallam Street as the year came in to the strains of "Ta-ra-ra-boom-de-ay" played by a piper from Beauly in striped trousers and a smoking jacket. All this brave show, however, was just a hollow mockery. There is no denying, now it is all over except the bandaging, that I was scared out of my wits most of the time. Just as Bernard Shaw used to hide his extreme shyness from the world behind a façade of flamboyant bombast, I concealed my craven soul beneath a mask of spurious gaiety like an old maid at a barn dance. But, to misquote Macbeth again, our present fears are often less than horrible imaginings, and when the day of dread came it turned out to be one of the most enjoyable in my life.

It began badly with a blinding snowstorm and a hopeless hunt for

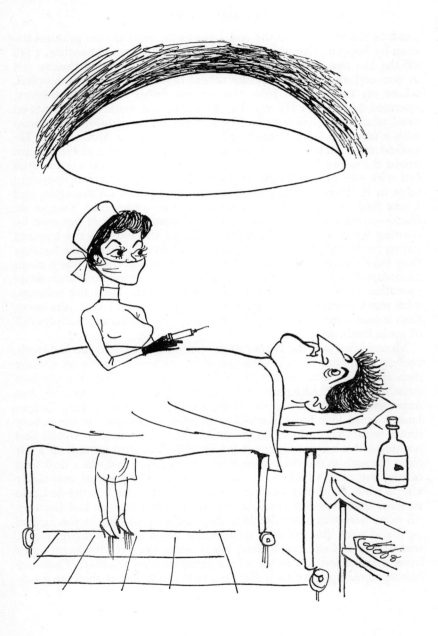

a cab in the blizzard. In the end I got to the hospital ten minutes too soon by hopping like a polar kangaroo from one bus to another. I fell off the last one into the slush and reached the operating theatre wet at one end and petrified at the other. It was St. George's hospital, where my countryman John Hunter, the father of modern surgery, operated on George III and Dr. Johnson, and made experiments on dead whales and live lizards. My surgeon was a handsome Irishman with a face like Gary Cooper and a voice like John McCormack. He wished me a Happy New Year, very much, I thought, as Pierrepoint might do to one of his customers, and showed me into a grim little cell with one blinding light and a narrow, leather-covered operating table in it. There was a grey blanket but no pillow on the table, and I was told by a pretty, rosy-cheeked nurse—rather like Yvonne de Carlo—to lie back and relax on it. She soon put me at my ease by pouring what seemed like gallons of liquid cocaine into my eye and telling me in a chatty sort of way that she didn't like Scotsmen because they were too cautious. All I could say to that was that it was a mean advantage to say a thing like that to a Scot after lashing him down on an operating table and filling him up with cocaine. Then the surgeon, who was evidently a traditionalist, told me it would hurt him more than it would me, and proceeded to pump my eyelids and temples full of some fresh drug.

Meanwhile from the corner of my sound eye I could see his lovely acolyte arranging rows of savage-looking glittering things on a silver dish and then, after asking me if I could feel anything, the surgeon switched on a blinding ray and I knew my hour had come. My last impression, I remember, before the job began was that Gary Cooper looked more like Boris Karloff as he slowly swooped at me upside down with that hideous knife in his hand. He said I would feel nothing but a heavy tugging at my eye-lid. And sure enough all I felt right through as the knife groped about inside my eye was a dull kind of tug, tug, tug, which was, oddly enough, quite pleasant and tickly after a while. With my weather eye I kept winking at Yvonne de Carlo to show that, however cautious her Scottish boy friends had been up till now, here was a regular Rob Roy laughing ha! ha! in the face of peril and pain. But before I could settle down to enjoy it properly it was all over and she was flushing my bleeding eye out with warm water from a queer looking bottle like a Spanish wine bladder. Then she bandaged me up, gave me a chit for a bottle of lotion, wished me good-morning and said "Next, please" to a terrified old man just as if she were a lady barber.

The whole thing took less than half an hour. Long before I am usually out of bed I was sitting in the Lyons teashop in Knightsbridge, like a snowman with my mane of bandages, eating one of Mr. Webb's sausages. And I looked disdainfully out of my one contemptuous eye at the cold and colourless crowd of clerks and watchmakers around me, who didn't have as much as a piece of sticking plaster to show between them. Thank you, Mr. Bevan, thank you, Gary Karloff, and God bless you, Yvonne de Carlo.

*January 4th*, 1951

## MY RUNCIBLE HAS ARRIVED !

THOSE of you who may recall my cri de cœur a few months ago will be pleased to hear the runcible hat has arrived at last. And what a lid it is! Such a topper has never been worn by mortal man before. It is a marvellous, magical and incomparable hat the like of which has never been seen since the Grand Panjandrum used to run around with the little round button on top. From now on I shall never be seen without it. I shall wear it morning, noon and night, waking and sleeping. Tomorrow, whatever the law or the registrar may say, I intend to be married in it. And when the time comes and I am summoned to Paradise I shall enter through the Pearly Gates with it on.

For this is no ordinary lid. It has been specially made out of moths wings and moonbeams and sent to me in a beautiful moonlight-coloured band-box by the great Mr. Battersby himself. I cried, you may remember, "Forward Mr. Battersby." And, unlike the spirits in the vasty deep who ignored Glendower's command, Mr. Battersby came forward with my hat in his hand. Perhaps it would be better to let Mr. Battersby describe this marvellous creation himself. The Battersbys, he points out proudly, have been making hats since 1865 and during that time have made many useful improvements on Edward Lear's original runcible. When you come to think of it Mr. Lear told us nothing about his hat except that he wore it and that he had a runcible spoon to go with it. Mr. Battersby's runcible is more substantial than that. "For instance," he explained, "the runcible hat we are sending you has an automatic oscillating debunker which is activated by an electronic toggle switch coupled to a secondary impulse regenerator." And he adds that as runcible hats can easily be ruined by inexpert treatment I should always send it back to Battersby's when anything goes wrong with the toggle. Needless to say, I am flattered to receive this remarkable hat from the maestro himself.

I shall take the greatest care of it in all winds and weathers and never leave the switch on when the hat is off. There has been nothing like it since the idrotobolic hat which was worn by the mashers at the great exhibition in 1851. That was a scientific topper with air valves and perspiration conductors in the lining. The only historic hats to compare with my new runcible, except Mr. Lear's, are "Beachcomber's" little round wickerwork hat and the famous copatain hat which Vincentio throws in Tranio's teeth in "The Taming of the Shrew." There is one feature of my hat, however, that outstrips all these and leaves even Lear's far behind running off with the runcible spoon. *My hat is invisible!* Not even I can see it. For, as Mr. Battersby explains in a note I found at the bottom of the hat box, "The best runcibles, being five-dimensional, can be perceived only by the intellect, and the clarity of the perception is dependent on the magnitude of the intellect."

That, perhaps, is why my friends have not yet noticed any difference in me. So far, like Macbeth's air-drawn dagger, it is but a headgear of the mind. But the thing will gradually appear like the Cheshire Cat as the intellects around me expand. Meanwhile, my new hat has one advantage which will be a great help to me in saloon bar parliaments from now on. I can now bet my opponents that I will eat my hat if I am wrong without having to sit down to a dish of velour goulash or Homburg thermidor as a Dewey supporter in Kansas had to do when Truman romped home two years ago.

*March 15th,* 1951


## ANTI THE ANTIS

IT has always seemed to me a great pity that when "Saki," the story-teller, died, nothing more was heard of his famous Anti-Luncheon League. For there was something about it, in spite of its name, that is missing from most of the other societies and associations which flourish on organised negation. In its way it was just as logical as the Anti-Liquor League. Its aim was to stop people eating as the aim of the prohibitionists is to stop them drinking. And I sometimes wonder if it would not have been better for the world if these two noble conceptions had been combined triumphantly in the late Victorian decades when most of our present mischiefs were growing in the smug, self-satisfied suburbs in an atmosphere of plush-framed photographs and aspidistras.

The Anti-Luncheon League was a simple little society. A small quarterly subscription entitled you to go without 92 luncheons. This meant that a paid-up member could go without 368 luncheons in a full year. Presumably—for they were never properly explained—the three extra meals you were allowed to go without covered leap year and enabled adventurous members to cross the international dateline without taking lunch. This happy league of abstinence seems to have been forgotten when its creator died, but a great idea of that kind is never entirely lost.

I was reminded of it the other day in Musselburgh, of all places, when a man, who had evidently been to the races, suddenly confronted me and in terrifying tones told me to beware of the wrath to come and join the anti-drink league. He was a haggard man with a theatrical air, and he carried in front of him a kind of tabard inscribed with lurid slogans calling attention to the perils of alcohol and the fate that lay in store for me if I ignored his advice. There was a glint in his eye which warned me he was not to be trifled with. And I prepared myself for the dialectical onslaught very much as Crito and his cronies must have resigned themselves to it when Socrates, driven out of the house by Xantippe's flying saucepans, bore down upon them. But before he cornered me he was driven from the field by a one-man band who played "The Road to the Isles" on a mouth-organ and a number of fierce percussion instruments attached to various parts of his body.

Before he disappeared, however, he shoved a leaflet into my hand which turned out to be a general denunciation of most of the activities of mankind. It was written in great, rolling sentences of almost Miltonic grandeur and informed me that in addition to his anti-liquor activities he was also the champion of various other organisations for the suppression of vice, vaccination, vivisection, Sunday cinemas, religious education, the colour-bar, stag-hunting, capitalism, Communism and the Pope. Like the drunken juror in "Blanco

Posnet" he was agin everything and I have no doubt when there is nothing else for him to be against he will turn his guns on himself.

I was sorry to lose him so soon after making his acquaintance for he was a man after my own heart, a brother to Socrates, Peter the Hermit, Voltaire and Swift, and to my own patron saint, St. Simeon Stylites, who was so much agin everything that he spent the last 33 years of his life on top of a pillar outside the racecourse at Antioch, where the people apparently were just as heedless of his maledictions as the folks at Musselburgh were of my friend's warnings the other afternoon. But his fleeting passage was not entirely in vain. For when he had gone the thought crossed my mind that nearly all the best people in the world so far have been cranks like him who were opposed to something or other. And, on balance, the Antis have done much greater good in the world than the Pros.

Taking things by and large it is the positive and not the negative people who create the major mischiefs. Nearly all wars and tyrannies are caused by people who want to do things and peace has nearly always to be restored by the negative people who stop them doing it. Nobody would deny, for instance, that it is better to be anti-cannibalistic than to be a cannibal, and, though I am on more dangerous ground here, it is probably better on the whole to be an anti-Disestablishmentarian, even if that is only an establishmentarian writ large. At all events I always feel more at home with people who are against something than I do with people who are always trying to impose something or other on me. In a queer kind of way, too, it is the Antis who make more converts to the things they oppose than the people who believe in them.

Be that as it may, my encounter with the anti-liquor man did me a lot of good. For I found on reading his pamphlet more carefully that he was not opposed to liquor in general but only to the kind of liquor that is called nowadays somewhat flatteringly "strong." His case against it was so strong that it had the effect on me that you probably expect, and when I got back to Edinburgh I went in to the old inn where Burns once lived and read his leaflet all over again over a pint of strong Scotch ale. And as I did so I pondered the possibility of co-ordinating all these negations and forming a new Anti-Anti Society in which they would all be united in one universal revolt against everything, even against being against anything.

*September 1st,* 1951

28

# I BECOME A REGULAR IRREGULAR

DURING my first half century on this distracted globe I have been a member of all sorts of queer clubs and strange societies. Almost as soon as I could walk I joined the Band of Hope and was publicly presented in a sailor suit as a brand from the burning, midst a great tremor of trombones and tambourines. On that occasion I sang "My drink is water bright" and made solemn pledges concerning my future consumption of liquids which, I'm afraid, have been more honoured in the breach than in the observance.

For an inglorious week or so I was a private in the Boys' Brigade. But owing to my unorthodox views on discipline I had to hand back my pill-box hat and shiny satchel and turn my infant mind to Shakespeare and Thucydides instead of forming fours and making sheepshank knots. This was all for the best for, when the time came, I learned to form fours in a harder school and so far I have never needed to make a sheepshank. Then I became a member of the Conservative Club in a northern city until they found out that most of the members were Socialists and cleared us all out. Even now, though I have quite a good home to go to, I am an incorrigible joiner of things. You have only to put a membership form in front of me and I will sign it.

I am a member of nearly twenty clubs and coteries, including the Society for the Flattening out of Switzerland and the "And Coal" Club, a secret society of Labour leaders and Pressmen which is so esoteric that even Transport House doesn't know what we stand for. But of all the things I have joined there is none I am more astonished to belong to than the Musgrave Ritualists of New York, to which I have just been elected as a lover of Sherlock Holmes.

For years I have studied the sacred writings and I have read everything ever written about the Master and his simple but indomitable stooge. I have been a vague unpaid-up member of the Baker Street Irregulars and I never pass through the old street without turning into Sherlock Holmes Mews down which Holmes and Watson crept on that enchanted and immortal night when Holmes came back from the dead to put the kybosh on Sebastian Moran in the Empty House. And only a year ago I went down river with Christopher Morley, the founder of the Irregulars, over the very waters where the Andaman Islander blew the poisoned darts at Holmes as he raced after him down Gallions Reach.

Until now, however, I have not been a regular Irregular but only a hanger-on. That is over now. My apprenticeship is ended and I am in the charmed circle at last. My membership form, which came the other day, says in simple but magical words that "Ian Mackay, having paced all the steps of the Sacred Ritual, is now a member in good standing of the Venerable Brotherhood of the Musgrave Ritualists of New York, the Scion Society of the Baker Street Irregulars." It is signed "Nathan L. Bengia, Keeper of the Crown," and dated "Anno Domini 1951, Anno Holmes 98."

What a wonderful way to start the New Year! I could not be more delighted if the King had made me a Knight of the Thistle or Colonel Rait Kerr had sent me a season ticket for the Tavern at Lord's. One of these days when I have enough dollars I will go to New York to claim my robes and go through my paces once more. Do you remember the Musgrave Ritual? "North by ten and by ten, East by five and by five, South by two and by two, West by one and by one, and so under." If my memory serves me that should land me up between Mr. Winchell and Tallulah in the Stork Club.

When I get there I shall join as well the Speckled Band of Boston, the Red Headed League of Pittsburgh, the Dancing Men of Denver, the Noble Bachelors of Scranton, the Crooked Men of Cleveland and the Scandalous Bohemians of Philadelphia. What a lecture tour the British Council could make of that. If they want me I am prepared to go even if I have to wear an Inverness cape and deerstalker and smoke a curved pipe.

But that, as Holmes would say, is only a pipe dream. What interests me most is that date, "Anno Holmes 98." It means the maestro will be 100 next year. He is I believe still hale, if not so hearty, since Watson passed away from the delayed effects of that extraordinary Afghan bullet which struck him in the shoulder and the groin at the same time. He passes the time away with his bees in the summer and on winter nights the shepherds on the Sussex Downs can hear him scraping away at the old Stradivarius.

When Chris Morley comes over next year we will go down together to Lewes to pay our respects to the old man. And who knows, we may even prevail upon him to emerge from retirement for a day or two to clear up the mystery of the Abominable Snowman and tell us what has happened to all that red meat we were promised a month or two ago.

*January 15th*, 1952

## THIS MADE ME FEEL BIGGER

MANY people—even some who have never been within a hundred miles of Charing Cross—must have felt a warm glow of self-satisfaction when they read that, in spite of all her trials and tribulations, London is still the biggest city in the world. Even I felt proud about it, though I am only a sudeten Londoner, a cuckoo in the Cockney nest as you might say. There was never any doubt that London was largest in size. For New York is a perpendicular town with its head in the clouds where men and women live in eyries like eagles and marmosets. And the claim of Los Angeles that it begins at the Columbia River and ends on the Mexican border is just a piece of Hollywood hyperbole. What pleased me was to hear that London is not only biggest in size, but in population as well. Despite all that has happened to her there are still half a million more people in London than there are in New York and twice as many as in Tokio and Moscow, the next on the list.

Usually I am not impressed by things merely because they are big. In fact, I avoid everything big from hotel bills to hangovers. A wren is no worse off because it is not an albatross and a fish is no better off in the Mississippi than it would be in the Windrush. Hamlet who thought that ripeness is all, summed it all up when he said he could be bounded in a nutshell and count himself a king of infinite space. Though I love London I sometimes long for some cosier corner deep in the green country where I could dream the days away among the murmuring bees, sup my ale in the cool twilight, sleep the night through in an apple-scented attic with the owls glimmering like ghosts in the garden and let the rest of the world go by. But that mood soon passes when I smell the asphalt burners in the Strand. When you scratch a Scot you find a Cockney even if we don't all wear our old clan ties like Mr. Morrison. So when I read that London is still the world's greatest town my heart leapt up as Wordsworth's did when he beheld the daffodils.

For the rest of the week I walked about the town with springs in my heels and when I meet my American friends in the Cheshire Cheese I look them in the eye and say, "Whaur's your Manhattan noo?" When you come to think of it this foolish pride in bigness is one of the queerest of human failings. Nobody ever wants to be the biggest

man—still less the biggest woman—in the world. Daniel Lambert grew till he was nearly half a ton, but who envied him as he puffed and blew his way from his tiny cradle to his gigantic grave? And I would lay you Blackpool Tower to a toothpick that Jolly Alice, the largest girl in the world, would swop places with the scraggiest millgirl who glowers at her if she had half a chance. Every year men and women spend millions on slimming tablets, taking the waters and doing their daily dozens. There is hardly any pain or discomfort they would shirk to prevent themselves getting big. Yet when it comes to cities we are all for municipal elephantiasis. Why the millions who squash and scramble through the traffic morning, noon and night to keep London going should be pleased about it is hard to understand, but we do.

Relatively speaking it doesn't matter much if a thing is big or little against the awful background of infinity. Out there above the village steeple behind the back of beyond, so far away that light moving at eleven million miles a minute takes millions of years to reach us, there are unseen universes so vast that they would swallow up every star we see as the universe we live in swallows up the atoms in a grain of sugar. And at the other end of the scale in the midget madhouse of the atom there are things so small that you could pack as many of them in a pin's head as there are sands on all the shores of the world. It is big whichever way you look at it. And the last of the ironies which must make all the devils dance in hell is that owing to the cleverness of wise men the tiny atom has become the biggest thing of all. For my part, I am all for moderation in these things. I stick to the wild absurdity of being normal, like that fantastic man in Barnum's Circus who was exactly 5ft. 8ins. high and claimed to be the smallest giant in the world and the largest dwarf. All the same, it's fun to live in little old London, big as it is.

*July 15th,* 1950

## NOW, IF GREENGAGE JAM WERE RED

THERE were, *mirabile dictu,* as Mr. Belloc would say, four different kinds of jam on the table in the train coming down from Scotland the other day—two red, one yellow and one green, to say nothing of the marmalade, which was in a separate dish all by itself, beside the little steel bracket in which the half-bottle of Medoc or Macon usually stands. "Ah," I said to myself, as Mr. Squeers did when he tasted the skimmed milk in the Saracen's Head in Snow Hill, "here's richness," and like that amiable and immortal monster, I smacked my lips and reached for the bread and butter.

It gave me quite an old-fashioned feeling to see such a brave profusion in so unlikely a place. And as I munched my toasted teacake and watched the sun shimmering on Scafell and the Langdale Pikes, and scattering diamonds over Morecambe Bay, the thought came into my head that, maybe, these four pots of British Railways jam were the first fragrant harbingers of the new Elizabethan age. They were not, perhaps, to be compared to the "sweet jams meticulously jarred" that the Bagdad grocers sold on the Golden Road to Samarkand which Flecker tells us were eaten by God's own prophet in Paradise, or even to that mellifluous mirage in Alice in Wonderland of which there was plenty yesterday and will be plenty tomorrow but never any today. Nor, so far as I could make out from their modest labels, did any of them claim royal patronage or wear a little badge saying it was "as supplied to the House of Lords" or even, as a tin of sardines I bought in Marseilles once boasted in golden gothic letters— "to the late Queen of Portugal."

But it was not the quality of the jam—though that was good enough —that impressed me so much as its variety. Even Lucullus himself, while he might have used some harsh words about the pie we had for lunch, could have had little complaint about the jam. Apart from the marmalade, which I might have expected to find on a train coming from Dundee, there were four full fruit jams, strawberry, apricot, blackcurrant and greengage, each in a fine fat shiny jar just like the one I used to keep my tadpoles and sticklebacks in in the days when bread and jam—but very seldom butter—were the twin staffs of my young life. Confronted with such unexpected riches, I found it hard to choose. For one wild Chestertonian moment I thought of taking a spoonful from each jar and mixing them up on my plate as Rembrandt used to mix his paints on his palette. But there was a whalebony woman opposite me watching with a cold subaqueous eye, and my courage oozed away. My nerve went completely when the waiter asked me which I would have and I pounced pusillanimously on the nearest jar, which turned out to be greengage.

This was the chance he was waiting for. "Wouldn't you rather have some strawberry or blackcurrant, sir?" he asked, and there was more than a touch of admonishment in his voice. He regarded me, I'm afraid, very much as the waiter at Southend regarded Sarah Bernhardt when she waved away the oysters and told him to bring her a large plate of cockles. This put me on my mettle. From that moment I was a greengage addict. I told him that I chose the greengage because I was wild about it and could not get it at all in my London suburb, where there are plenty of rich red, black, pink and yellow jams but no green ones. Normally I adopt the same attitude towards greengage jam that I did towards plum and apple when I was in the Army. But I was not to be ordered about or even cajoled by the hotels executive.

Like the king in Mr. Milne's poem who was determined to get a little bit of butter for his bread and would not be put off with marmalade I stood firm. Or, rather, I sat firm and smeared the hideous concoction on my bread and my bun at least an inch thick. Though I was dying for a juicy spread of strawberry, I went on gobbling greengage just to show them—particularly the valkyrie with the swordfish eyes—that I was master of the situation. Whether they were impressed or not I shall never know, for waiters rarely give themselves away even when they are going at 80 miles an hour, and there was nothing to be read in that cold, colourless eye opposite me. So when the greengage was all gone I settled down in my corner and watched England reeling out behind me into the thickening night.

As we clattered along past Newton-le-Willows and through the grimy wilderness of Warrington, I pondered on the mystery of colour and wondered why a strawberry should be red while a greengage was green. Then I began to let my fancy roam and I thought what a shock it would be to the world if we woke up one morning and found all the colours had got mixed up in the night. What, I wondered, would happen if all the milk was red and the coffee green? And how would we like it if, when we ordered a porterhouse steak and onions, the steak turned out to be blue and the onions crimson? Some years ago, I reminded myself, a brewer tried to popularise green beer, but nothing came of it. He might as well have tried to sell black whisky. Maybe if somebody would dye greengage jam to look like strawberry I might get to like it. But as long as it looks like pulped cabbage I will never be fond of it, even though I bolt it down in great dollops to show the hotels executive who is boss.

*March 1st, 1952*

35

4

## YES, OF COURSE I'M SUPERSTITIOUS

ALTHOUGH there are still some people left who are convinced the earth is flat, and a few even who think there is a real man in the moon, it is still a surprise to me when I come across somebody who really believes that black cats bring good luck, and that to spill the salt means misfortune. No amount of science or schooling seems to have any effect on these foolish, but harmless, superstitions, which are based on something much deeper than knowledge or reason, or even than faith itself. For it is part of the endless mystery of the mind that it holds more firmly to these deep irrational things than it does to the things on the surface that can be proved. And the odd thing about it is, that whilst I laugh at these nonsensical notions about black cats, spilt salt and cross-eyed chimney sweeps, I half believe in them myself. When it comes to picking pins up or not walking under ladders I am as irrational as the great logician Jevons, who believed that unemployment was caused by sun-spots.

While I do not go as far as one of my old Fleet Street colleagues, who used to leave his spectacles at home when there was a new moon, so that he would not see it first through glass, I always turn my money over when I see that silver shaving in the sky. Fortunately, there is no harm in these foolish fancies, and I am glad to think they are shared by most of my fellow-mortals. When I visited the Vatican last year the place was full of ladders, and I noticed with a good deal of Presbyterian satisfaction, that a swan-like covey of American nuns who were being shown round, took great care not to walk under them. This pleased me very much as I had done a lot of ladder-dodging that morning myself, and I came away wondering if the Pope shared our human frailty in this respect. When he upsets the salt, as he must do now and then with those long sleeves of his, does His Holiness throw a pinch furtively over his shoulder when the Swiss Guard are not looking? And does he always take care never to invite 12 Cardinals to dinner?

These idle speculations about superstition came into my mind the other day when I went to a luncheon party in honour of Randolph Turpin and found myself sitting next to a man who turned out to be an Aristotelian empiricist. He believed, he told me, in nothing that cannot be proved by experiment, and, for that reason he was inclined to doubt such things as the quantum theory, or that space and time are just two aspects of the same thing. He was particularly sceptical about the modern system of measuring stellar distances in light-years, and refused point-blank to believe that the light of the Pole Star that we see tonight, left there before William the Conqueror was born.

There are sound scientific reasons for believing these things, but my Aristotelian friend would not accept them without, what he called, absolute proof. He was just telling me he could not even accept the atomic theory of matter when he knocked over the salt. It would not be true to say he went pale, but it stopped his speech almost as if he had been shot. He solemnly gathered a large pinch of the salt and threw it over his shoulder, murmuring some incantation as he did so. When I chaffed him about it he laughed a little sheepishly and said "that" was different. Then he told me that, in spite of Aristotle, he also believed that if you place a poker across the bars of the grate it will make the fire burn better. This, he explained is because it forms the Sign of the Cross, which drives the Devil away. I could not resist pointing out to him that if he wanted a good blaze the Devil was the last person he should drive away. But when I reflected on it afterwards I wondered why I made fun of the inconsistent empiricist.

Only the other night when I travelled up to Scotland I was relieved to note that there are only 12 compartments in each sleeping car. It was quite refreshing, in fact, to find that even such an impersonal body as British Railways is based on sound superstitious foundations. At all events, I intend to go on believing in some of these foolish things. For I believe, with Bacon, that the greatest superstition of all is to go out of your way to avoid superstition. It may be, in the end, that the legends and superstitions will outlast the logics and the sciences, and that, even when we conquer the space-time continuum and reach beyond Betelgeuse a billion years from now, there will still be men walking round ladders. Anyway, I intend to be on the safe side, and when I spill the salt this evening—as I am sure to do—I shall throw a little over my shoulder and tell the Devil in all friendliness, to go to Hades where he belongs.

*March 29th,* 1952

37

## ME AND MY PEN

A VERY unusual and, in its way, alarming thing happened to me on Thursday morning when I sat down to write this piece. I found I had nothing to write it with. As there were no newspapers to be produced for Friday I thought it would be a good thing to stay at home for a change and do my work in the garden among the brisk orange-billed blackbirds. I rigged up a wicker-work table on the sunny side of the house and, with a glass of Beaujolais to lend warmth and colour to my fancy, I sat me down beside a bed of dying daffodils to write "something for the paper."

This is always a great moment in an essay writer's life. It is what the bullfighters call the moment of truth when the writer, however exalted or humble he may be, is left alone with the stubborn bull of his imagination and something must be done about it. And when the essay is for a newspaper the moment cannot be shirked or postponed, for the crowd is, as it were, already in the arena, and no matter how miserable the Fleet Street matador may be or how wild and intractable the bull, the show must go on. But the most daring and accomplished of matadors, even the great Manolete himself, could do little without their swords.

When I squared up for the kill, so to speak, I looked round for my espada—my faithful fountain pen which has tamed many a recalcitrant bull in its time—but it was nowhere to be found. I hunted high and low, even in such unlikely places as the coalshed and the clock, but there was no sign of it. In the end I gave up the search and hoped I had left it in the office among the old Hansards and the invitations to visit book clubs and open bazaars. Now this was a serious matter for me as I can no longer write with a lead pencil as I did when I was an honest reporter. And though I can tap out "Annie Laurie" and "Some Enchanted Evening" on the piano with one finger I have never been able to master the complicated contraption which the French call the writing machine.

There were plenty of things in my head when I sat down beside the daffodils, and I had even arranged some of them in decent order. I meant to write about the old lady who died in her shoes because she would wear them on the wrong feet. This, it seemed to me, was an admirable subject for a short, moralising, but not too serious disquisition on queer habits and customs. But when I found that my pen was missing I could not write a line. I was flummoxed.

My wife has a much more magnificent pen than mine, a glittering sylph with a jewelled hood and gold waistcoat as if it were dressed by Dior, far too opulent an aristocrat to mix with my poor snub-nosed manual labourer with its broken cap and leaky joints. I tried to make a start with this bauble but it was all in vain. I called my spirits from the vasty deep but they would not come. So I just sat and stared at the paper, and all my fancies fled like a flock of starlings when a car backfires. This tyrant custom, which brought down Othello, is a terrible thing and it baffled me as well. In the end I took a cab to Fleet Street to get my pen which cost me the price of at least two new pens and half a hundred pencils.

I had to do it, for without my pen I am as tongue-tied as Lord Balfour is said to have been at a banquet when he wore Court dress and had no lapels to hang on to when he got up to speak. I am pernickety, too, about my ink. It must be blue, the lighter blue the better, and even then I can only write on white paper. Call me a creature of habit if you will, like the old lady who could only walk with her shoes on the wrong feet. I can't help it. I am, as Descartes said, because I think I am. And as nobody else can think *me* for *me* I must put up with it and put my best foot foremost even if my shoes are on the wrong feet.

Me and my old pen must make the best of it till the day comes when I lay it up for the last time and leave the bulls to bellow in some younger head. Whoever that head may belong to I hope he will use a pen, too, and leave the writing machines to the lost souls who write about Antofogastas and Consols. It is the only way of writing for the likes of them.

*April 12th,* 1952

## PART OF ME HAS GONE WITH BERT

TO many men and women of my generation who still imagine they are at the high noon of their existence, or, at any rate, a long way from what Macbeth called the sere and yellow, it must have been an unpleasant surprise to learn that Ella Shields was a great-grandmother. For I have always looked upon Burlington Bertie as a contemporary of mine, the kind of chap I might have been if I had been unlucky enough to be born at the top with nowhere to go but down instead of at the bottom with nowhere to go but up. He was very much a type of his time and I thought his time was mine. How was I to know when I first saw Burlington Bertie come toddling on like a toff at the Edinburgh Empire more than thirty years ago that he was already an old roué, and that he was walking down the Strand with his gloves in his hand long before I left school? Time, that inexorable and insatiable cormorant, has no right to play tricks with us like that.

Fancy the shock, therefore, when I discovered that Bertie was the last of the dandies, a contemporary of such immortal spirits as the Lily of Laguna, the Man That Broke the Bank at Monte Carlo, the Young Lady Who Wouldn't Leave Her Little Wooden Hut for Anybody and her more accommodating sister Daisy who is, I am happy to say, still pedalling to paradise every night in almost every public-house, on her bicycle built for two. The last time I saw Ella Shields was at the Metropolitan in Edgware Road two years ago when she took part in that orgy of nostalgia called Thanks for the Memory. It was hard to believe when she came on, to the old familiar strain, that when she first appeared there Dan Leno, Marie Lloyd and the White-Eyed Kaffir were on the bill with her, Walter Sickert was in the bar sketching the stage through the glass window and Max Beerbohm was in the stalls looking terribly like the chap Burlington Bertie would have been if he had kept to the straight and narrow path. There were no aeroplanes, films, radio, motor buses or aspirins in those days. It was an easy pleasant carefree world in which everything seemed fixed for all time. The Peacemaker was on his throne, the pound was still looking the dollar in the face rather like an old dowager looking down her nose at a chorus girl and there were plenty of people hungry and unemployed, though nobody had started counting them yet.

No doubt when I first heard Bert confessing across the footlights that night in Edinburgh that he hadn't a shirt I took it as a joke just as I accepted George Carney's declaration that he landed with William the Conk and Marie Lloyd's announcement that she was one of the ruins that Cromwell knocked about a bit. All that was far away and long ago. It is easy, looking back with the Beveridge Report and the Welfare State in mind, to see that things were not nearly so funny for Bertie as they sounded in the warm, ginny atmosphere of the Empire Music Hall. But I can see now that Burlington Bertie was, in his way, just as much a forerunner of the revolution that has taken place in Britain as Chekov's tramp in "The Cherry Orchard" was the advance agent of Lenin and Trotsky. Maybe that is why Burlington Bertie has outlived so many of his more fashionable contemporaries. For a comic character to live it seems that he must be a little bit tragic, like Falstaff, Don Quixote and Mr. Chaplin's tramp, who I am glad to see still survives, no matter how many new suits and top hats his creator may provide for him.

When a great character like Ella Shields dies it is a personal matter for all of us. For part of ourselves dies too. Such persons are woven into the pattern of their time and when they die a little of ourselves goes with them. When Marie Lloyd died I stood in the crowd in the Finchley Road and cried like a child as everybody else did too. There was no special reason why everybody in that vast throng should have cried. As Hamlet said of the player, what's Hecuba to him or he to Hecuba that he should mourn her thus. And there was no reason in Paris the other day when I heard that Ella Shields had gone why I should have felt so sad and gone home feeling that something had gone from the sky. She meant no more to me than Marie Lloyd had done, or for that matter than Shakespeare and Socrates do today. But I cried all the same. I can see now that this was selfish and vain of me. For it was Burlington Bertie I was crying for. For he had become part of the fabric of my life—even if only a little part—and I was crying because part of me was dead.

*August 9th,* 1952

## MR. WEEKLEY NAMES MY SECRET VICE

THOUGH I have, so far, managed to keep it dark, I have known for a long time that I am a grangeriser. I have known, too, that I am a serendipidist, a deisnosophist and, as my friends in the Marble Bar, Newcastle, can vouch for, a malakoffian of considerable promise. But, until I dipped into Ernest Weekley's new edition of his famous Concise Etymological Dictionary of Modern English I had no idea that I was a grahamiser as well. Or, that in my youth, when I had the run of a druggist's shop, I was a galingale consumer on a gargantuan scale.

Before explaining all this mumbo-jumbo, I must advise you all to get hold of this stimulating, exotic, exciting and permanently important book by fair means or foul. For you will be astounded, as you skim through it, to find out how many queer things you have been in your time without knowing it. My own past, I need hardly tell you, is not nearly so murky as it sounds. A grangeriser is a common enough kind of chap—a mutilator of books. A serendipidist is one who finds one thing when he is looking for another. A deisnosophist is a regular diner-out. And, as every denizen of the Marble Bar knows, a mala-koffian is one who takes part in a four-handed game of dominoes. I am fairly good at all these things, though my chances of indulging in any of them are not as frequent as they used to be.

It was a shock, however, to discover that for many years I have been a secret grahamiser. According to Mr. Weekley, this means an opener of other people's letters. This, I hasten to assure the Post-master-General—who was a left-wing Socialist when I last met him—does not mean that I am the leader of the mail-bag robbers' ring. But as soon as I see an envelope on my desk I have to open it. It is an irresistible impulse, like Sarah Bernhardt's habit of touching sailors' collars in the street. I have a device on my desk for pasting them up again and a special stamp expressing my regret.

It is nice to feel one is a grahamiser and not just a common Paul Pry. The name derives from an almost forgotten countryman of mine, who was Home Secretary under Peel. He became very unpopular with the Liberals for opening Mazzini's letters in the post. This was very naughty of him, no doubt, but it is odd to think that, though he is forgotten as one of the framers of the Reform Bill, he will always be remembered, in this queer way, because he opened Mazzini's mail.

How was I to know when I swiped the Chinese ginger in the back shop that I was a galingale addict? Chinese ginger, by any other name, tastes just as sweet when you can get it. And I am not nearly as astonished to hear I was eating galingale as the man in Moliere's play was to learn he had been speaking prose all his life. But I was surprised to learn that a paddymelon is a kangaroo and a quagga a zebra, and that crivello was not an early Italian composer but an elephant's tusk weighing less than 20lb. Though I was once a Rechabite I had never heard of the Rebeccaites. They were, it seems, a mob of Welsh en-thusiasts who used to tear down turnpike gates in the name of the

Lord. You will find why they took the name in Genesis 24 and 50.

Then how was I to know that our old friend Sir Waldron, among his other accomplishments, is the last of the jusquaboutistes? They are the French equivalent of our last-ditch diehards. Nor did I know that clergymen's gowns—and barristers' too, for that matter—are made of prunella or that a Rob Roy is a canoe.

It was no news to me that a daltonist is not a man with a big voice and a song in his heart, but somebody—like Sir Walter Monckton and Mr. Justice Wethered, the conjuring judge—who suffers from colour blindness. There is no end to the terminological tit-bits in Mr. Weekley's lucky bag of words and phrases. Did you know, for example, that a remora is a sucking fish, a strigil a skin scraper, a sockdologer a knock-out blow, a teredo a boring shellfish and a trochilus a bird that lives by cleaning crocodiles' teeth?

Here and there I quarrel with Mr. Weekley. As, for instance, when he calls a loon a lout, and suggests Old Nick is based on the German word nickel, which means goblin. A loon, as Ramsay MacDonald was always pointing out, is merely, in Scotland, a young lad. Even I was a loon once. And I am sure that the original of Old Nick was Machiavelli, who was generally regarded during his lifetime—at all events in Scotland—as His Sulphuric Majesty in person. But these are minor matters. This is a thrilling and nourishing book which should certainly be in every serendipidist's home. But let the grangerisers keep their hands off it. It is a life-long treasure.

*August 21st, 1952*

## LAMENT FOR A FLY

A T first I thought it was the Hoover humming in the next room. There was just that drowsy, faraway buzz about it which always reminds me—when the vacuum cleaner is snuffling around the room —of my childhood days when I lay in bed with measles or mumps and the "Magnet" and listened to the wild whoops of my barbaric comrades chasing moths—we called them "story flies"—in the hawthorn-scented twilight or playing football with fishermen's corks in the moonlit meadow they call the Bleaching Green in Wick. This is the riverside lawn where Robert Louis Stevenson began to plant his Child's Garden of Verse and though later on—when he was in San Francisco—he called Wick the "meanest of men's towns on the baldest of God's bays," he always retained his boyhood love for the Green. But that is a nostalgic digression only excused by the fact that I was born on that Green, and the old lady who helped my mother to get me into the world used to give R. L. S. peppermints when he roamed romantically up that same riverside.

When I heard the old familiar hum yesterday morning I was more than half asleep, wallowing luxuriously in that delicious dreamland between the first and second awakening before the tigerspring of Monday morning clawed me back from the lazy paradise of a nihilistic week-end to the chains and slavery of Fleet Street. The soothing buzz nearly sent me off to sleep again, but when I looked at my watch I sat up with a start. It was only half-past seven, and Mrs. Wickens, who "does" for me three days a week, never turns up till ten. But the buzz-buzz went on, and I realised it was just by my ear.

Then I saw him. It was the last bluebottle of the year, and he was buzzing and bumping about the room as big and bouncy as a wren. My first wicked instinct was to get up and kill him, and I am ashamed to say I had one or two swipes at him with the *New Statesman*. The wind of one savage swish made him dance in the air like a dinghy in the wake of the Queen Mary. After that he—or maybe it was she—came to rest on top of volume six of Gibbons' "Decline and Fall." The poor thing was completely done in. I felt thoroughly ashamed of myself, threw the *New Statesman* into the fireplace, and opened the window wide to let the fly go free. In the end I had to shake Gibbon out of the window. The fly stuck grimly on but in the end I saw him spinning downwards for ten yards or so and then take to his wings again. He went off in the direction of China. Then with a rosy glow of self-righteousness flooding my soul, as if I were St. Francis of Assisi himself, I went and boiled myself a Polish egg and made a nice cup of tea.

And as I sat over the fire and listened to the 8-o'clock News I ruminated on the mystery of things. I recalled that terrifying tale by Katherine Mansfield in which she upsets the ink over a fly. She watched its struggles with the dreadful feeling that somewhere behind her at any moment some mightier being may wipe her out just as

blindly and aimlessly as she has drowned the fly. Then I looked up that tremendous passage in "Titus Andronicus" where Titus blames his brother for killing a fly. "But how," he asks, "if that fly had a father and a mother? How would he hang his slender gilded wings, and buzz lamenting doings in the air! Poor harmless fly, that, with his pretty buzzing melody, came here to make us merry! and thou hast kill'd him." All Marcus could say in reply was that it was a "black, ill-favour'd fly like to the empress' Moor." Not even a blue-bottle. Shakespeare had a weakness for flies and beetles. You may remember the overwhelming passage in "Measure for Measure"—perhaps the most stupendous statement in the whole of Shakespeare —where Isabella cries, "The poor beetle that we tread upon, in corporal sufferance finds a pang as great as when a giant dies." It must have been the memory of that that made me throw the "States-man" in the grate. But the great big world kept turning and I had to get ready for the road. And, as is the way of all humanitarians, I soon forgot all about my friend the bluebottle.

But this was not the last of him. When Mrs. Wickens came to clear away the crocks there he was dead as a doornail in the sugar-bowl. He must have staggered back somehow for one last orgy before passing away for ever into the flies' Valhalla. He was curled up in the bowl with the nodules of sugar clinging to his feelers, feet and wings. A sweet death. He could not have finished up better had he been one of Homer's—or was it Ovid's?—golden bees who died so mellifluously on Mount Hymettus. And if, as I suspect by his buzzing, bouncing and bumping, he was a Conservative bluebottle how fortunate it was for him to die just in time to be buried in Tate and not in State sugar.

*December 6th,* 1949


## IS THIS FORBIDDEN FRUIT?

FOR some weeks now I have been disturbed by one of those problems which, though they never seem to bother anybody who lives in the country, are always troubling the minds and con-sciences of the people who live in the towns. Stated in its crudest terms, my problem may be summed up in one simple question. Am I entitled to eat the apples and pears which fall into my garden from my neighbour's trees? As there are no fruit trees in my own garden I am compelled to admit that these apples and pears—which are very tasty by the way—do not belong to me. They undoubtedly come from my neighbour's trees which hang, like vast umbrellas, far over the garden wall. Somehow I feel guilty about them although, so far, I have accepted them in very much the same spirit in which the children of Israel accepted the manna which appeared so magically every morning like hoar-frost on the ground. The pears are not as sweet as they might be, but the apples might have been plucked by Atalanta herself. Each day before I leave for the City I collect this windfall and store it away in my cellar along with my meagre supply of wine. We have had two apple pies from it already and one plateful of stewed pears.

Nevertheless I am troubled about this forbidden fruit and sure I am doing wrong. For the Presbyterian conscience with which I embarked upon my earthly pilgrimage, though it is not nearly as hard a taskmaster as it was, still gives me an occasional touch of the lash, just to remind me that so far as the Auld Kirk is concerned there are no qualifications to the Eighth Commandment. Every morning this fruit is there in my garden, yet I feel, somehow, that the savage's rule that possession is nine points of the law is hardly applicable in the Welfare State, especially where your neighbour's apples are concerned. And, whilst I am a devout believer in Proudhon's axiom that all property is theft, I have gathered enough small gear of my own not to insist on its practical application, at any rate in postal district N.W.3.

My main trouble, however, is not so much ethical as topographical. My neighbour's garden is so much bigger than mine, and his house so far away that I have never seen him or it. For all I know he may be a Mongolian mandarin, or even one of those Shavian millionaires bowed down beneath the miserable weight of his possessions. Probably I shall never get to know him—if he is a he at all and not a country club or a sanatorium—and so I may have to go on eating his apples and pears as long as I live just over his garden wall. I could, of course, throw them all back over the wall, but as that would involve me in a great deal of manual labour I have ruled that solution of the problem right out. There is also the possibility if I start throwing these apples about that I may hit my mysterious neighbour with one of them and lay him out beside the lily pond like the squire in one of Mrs. Christie's whodunits. Just think of the confusion at Scotland Yard if he did turn

47

out to be a mandarin. But even if I missed him I might very well damage his glasshouses or poison his goldfish. Then what should I do if I was summoned for restoring his property to him the hard way?

There is still another course open to me. I could sue him for leaving his property lying about on my property. But as a Socialist this would mean admitting that I am a property owner. And goodness knows what trouble that would get me in with Mr. Bevan. At the same time it will be a fine state of affairs if I have to eat apple dumplings all through the winter to keep my land clear of his accursed pippins. As the Mackays have only one square yard of land left in their own country they are jealous of the little bits they have picked up in other parts of the world. One member of the clan has acquired the best part of Amsterdam and another owns a substantial slab of Broadway. Though I have little hope of emulating them, I have a small piece of rented land just big enough to hold a deck-chair, a wickerwork table, a portable wireless and a brace of budgerigars. It is long enough at one end for my neighbour's trees to sprawl all over me. At the other end there is no wall at all and on foggy nights the taxis come crawling on to my lilliputian lawn, very much as William the Silent's warships went crashing through the apple orchards of Holland, to surprise Alva at his revels, fifty miles from sea.

In the end I expect nothing will happen. I will go on eating his apples and, as he is so far away, he will never know anything about it. In this way something like justice will be done. For I shall consume in solid form in winter some of the sunshine his trees have robbed me of in summer. All the same, I wish I knew who he was. I should like to make some reparation to him, to throw him perhaps an occasional tin of oatcakes or a haggis. But it would be better to know who he is before I do that. I have a jar of Chinese ginger left in case he is a mandarin after all!

*September 20th*, 1952

# PART THREE

# 6-o'clock Deadline

## SOCRATES DEBUNKS FAIRIES

THAT upright and much maligned philosopher, the early Scrooge —before Dickens went sentimental and turned him into the smug, insufferable humbug who now presides with sickening eleventh-hour benevolence over our Christmas revels—would have enjoyed himself in our local tavern last night when the talk got round to pantomimes. When I got there a little late, laden with a fortnight's groceries which have been piling up during my Parisian exile, our leading orator, a regular Socrates of the sawdust bar, was in full spate tapping the table, waving his arms about, poking his pipe into everybody's ribs, and scattering tobacco ash in everybody's beer. There was that savage glitter in his eye which showed that he was stirred to the utmost depths of his soul. His theme was the Christmas pantomime, and when I arrived he was going for Cinderella.

Far from being the poor despised young victim of those hideous hags, the Ugly Sisters—whom I always think of as Naughton and Gold—she was, it seems, a nasty little snob who turned her back on honest work and fell for the spurious glamour and glitter of a princely and unmannerly prig who publicly humiliated her poor old sisters simply because they were ugly. He quoted copiously from one Sarah Trimmer a formidable foe of fairy tales who unmasked Cinderella as long ago as 1802.

This wicked tale, said Sarah—and I have looked it up, as the Speaker would say, for the purpose of greater accuracy—"paints in flattering colours some of the worst passions that can enter into the human breast, of which little children should be totally ignorant, such as envy, jealousy, vanity, and the love of dress, to say nothing of hatred of sisters and mothers-in-law." Socrates sank his pint, and after it was replenished turned the tirade on to Robinson Crusoe, whose evil example, he said, again citing the stern Sarah, "led young boys to

49

an early taste for a rambling life, and a vulgar desire for adventures."
It is Crusoe, in fact, who makes Bevin boys loathe the mines and
haberdashers run off to Patagonia. As for "Mother Goose," with its
fantastic nonsense about cows jumping over the moon and cats playing
fiddles, and "Jack and the Beanstalk," "that abominable absurdity,"
as the poet Bloomfield called it, he condemned them as intellectual
opium of the most pernicious kind which bemused the childish mind
and filled the imagination with a nonsensical farrago of supernatural
events of no social or spiritual significance whatever.

Even when I meekly interposed to report that only the day before,
in mid-Channel, I had actually seen scores of dishes running away
with scores of spoons, he was unshaken and turned his guns on Red
Riding Hood—"a silly little nincompoop who could not distinguish
between a wolf and her grandmother"—Puss in Boots—"that dis-
gusting biological monstrosity"—and Little Goldilocks who, he
maintained, was in reality a withered old crone from Connemara
called "Silver Hair." Then he returned with a sweeping swing of his
tumbler to "Cinderella," and triumphantly pointed out that the whole
story of the glass slipper was a lot of lies built up on a slipshod mis-
translation of Perrault's famous fairy tale.

The Frenchman apparently wrote that when she fled from the ball
at midnight Cinderella—he called her Cendrillon—dropped her
pantoufle en vair, which means slipper of fur or miniver. When this
reached the English translator, Robert Samber, he misread vair as
verre, and so for all time that slipper will be glass. Finally, he declared
with vicious glee, that the one fairy tale he is in favour of is "Babes in
the Wood" which finishes up in unrelieved misery and gloom, and
he sternly rebuked the shade of Sir Oswald Stoll who twisted the
whole thing so that it ended happily with the Babes singing away
lustily at each other among a bevy of Tiller robinettes.

Taking it by and large, I'm sure old Scrooge would have taken to
Socrates. He might even have agreed with his parting shot to me
that it would have been a good thing for every poor, harassed
parent if Dickens had stuck to founding the "Daily News" and
left Christmas where it was, away somewhere in the Bavarian
Alps.

*December 18th, 1946*

## GANGING AGLEY ON HOGMANAY

THE great and glorious thing about Hogmanay, if you happen to be a Scot, is that, no matter how sedately or with what lofty aspirations you may embark on that blessedly infrequent festival, there is no telling where you will find yourself before the night is out. I have known solemn men in spats, fathers of fond families, grown grey in the service of the State, veritable pillars of Presbyterian propriety, set forth from Surbiton or Crouch End upon that happy morn, with their minds full of noble thoughts, finish up in Vine Street sharing a cell with some verminous ruffian they would set the dog on if he dared to show his face at the door of Ben Nevis or The Cairngorms.

More than once, in my own modest way, I have seen the New Year in from some strange balconies and in some dubious dives, including one shameful occasion when I set out, disguised as Cyrano de Bergerac, to dance it in at the Chelsea Arts Ball and woke up shivering in a garage in Tiger Bay, Cardiff. And then there was the great night in Loos in 1916, when I dived down a hole to get away from a "Jack Johnson" and found myself in a kind of Ali Baba's cave, surrounded by rows of rum jars and sides of ham. With the unerring second sight of the Black Mackays, I had plunged straight as a plummet into the quartermaster's stores.

This year, determined so far as possible to preserve some sense of decency and decorum, I made arrangements to see the New Year in at home. The idea was to greet the newcomer in luxury, propped up in bed with Smollett in one hand and a goblet of something in the other, and to wish the whole world and his wife a happy and fruitful New Year—especially the "hundeserving," as Liza's father, old Doolittle, calls us. But alas, something went wrong as the evening shadows fell, and when the great moment came and the sirens began to scream over the river, I found myself on the balcony of Whistler's old tavern, the Angel, at Rotherhithe, bellowing "The Miner's Dream of Home" and waving a shadowy glass to the dim outline of an alert seaman on the bridge of a ghostly steamer as it slipped noiselessly past Wapping Old Stairs down Conrad's "dark river of the nine bends," on its way to what fragrant or fever-stricken shores none

51

of us could tell. But that sailorman waved back as the bells boomed over the immense city, and I wish him and his fine ship many happy landfalls and fair havens wherever they may go in the austere service of the sea.

It was here on this very balcony—they say you can still see the stains where he spilt his paints—that Turner first sought out the secrets of the sunset, and it was from here, too, that Whistler "flung a pot of paint in the face of the public," as Ruskin said in that unhappy phrase which cost him a farthing in the law courts and lost him the respect of all eternity. Legros, too, and Augustus John came here to this old riverside tavern, where once the press gang used to sandbag the local drunks into the Service so that Britannia might continue to rule the waves. Just across the stream we could hear the revellers in the inn near Execution Dock, where Captain Kidd concluded his career at the business end of a rope.

What a place this Rotherhithe is. From the days when King Canute held Court here right down to Ben Smith and the Tory who lost his deposit the other day, this fascinating London backwater has literally overflowed with history. Shakespeare, who called it Red Rose Haven, in all probability lived here. It was the Redriff of the "Beggar's Opera." King John did most of his wenching here before he got on the wrong side of the bourgeoisie. Captain Cook sailed from Rotherhithe. And it was on one of the Rotherhithe wharves that Sexton Blake and Tinker finally trapped that prince of master criminals, George Marsden Plummer. As the New Year began to stretch its infant limbs we could see Tower Bridge silhouetted against the rich glow of the roystering City and hear, coming up from St. Paul's, the rather terrifying hum of humankind as my sentimental countrymen roared their pagan choruses and cracked their bottles outside the parish church of London.

Eventually I got home, but I was too sleepy for Smollett, and I had scarcely touched the pillow before I was off, to be awakened four hours later with the glorious news that "Yardley had bowled *him*." May I finish by just wishing you all a very good New Year and may we all get better than we deserve, "else," as Shakespeare tells us, "who would 'scape whipping."

*January 2nd*, 1947

## THE GREAT M'GONAGALL

IT was one of our most assiduous back benchers—a smooth, squirmy, well-soaped sort of fellow—who came oozing oilily up to me outside the House of Lords yesterday afternoon and, after inquiring unctuously after my welfare and that of my non-existent family, reminded me that the world's greatest literary and alcoholic jamboree, Burns Nicht, is almost upon us once again. And there was a sly leer in his piggy little eye as he gave my arm a soft, pudgy squeeze, peered greasily up at me like a Port Said postcard pedlar, and sniggered "Old Bobbie is one of my favourite poets, a bit of a gay dog, too, in his day, wasn't he?" After that it was not surprising to find that he thought Burns wrote "I Love a Lassie" and "Bonnie Mary of Argyle," and before he got on to "I Belong to Glasgow" and "Stop Yer Ticklin' Jock" I slaked him off me and took refuge behind Rodin's masterpiece, "The Burghers of Calais," which I am glad to see back on its plinth beside Mrs. Pankhurst in Victoria Tower Gardens to remind the political misogynists in the House of Lords that on the whole the women of England have always been a lot better than her men. But before shaking him off I could not resist one final fling at him. So I told him that while I considered that Burns was a first-rate poet— if rather ragged and rough and ready at times—I thought it was a great pity that the brilliant blaze of his universal fame should have obscured, for later generations, the smaller but still passionate flame of that sweet but sadly neglected singer, the Great M'Gonagall, the Bard of the Silvery Tay.

William M'Gonagall, who was born in Edinburgh "of poor but honest Irish parents" in 1830, was much more of a modernist than Burns. His maidens were indeed all forlorn and frequently hard done by but, unlike most of Rabbie's girl friends, they never seem to have had any fun on the road to ruin. Every one of them, from the old Queen sulking behind the barricades and John Brown at Balmoral, down to the fisher lass keening over her drowned lover on the quayside at Dundee, is steeped in deep Æschylean gloom. Compared with the happiest of M'Gonagall's heroines Tess of the D'Urbervilles was as full of pep and gaiety as Carmen Miranda. Take the Duchess of Albany at the graveside of her husband, Prince Leopold, who M'Gonagall—a first-class reporter—is careful to point out was dead

53

before they buried him. "As she viewed her husband's remains," he writes, "it was really sublime.

"Her tears fell fast on the coffin lid without delay,
  Then she took a last fond look at him and hurried away."

But there was worse to come. When Queen Victoria turned up in her widow's weeds the Coldstream Guards had broken down and were crying like babies, while the Seaforth Highlanders who had the job of lowering Leopold into the tomb had "dissolved in tears."

Her Majesty herself had a tough time too. Let M'Gonagall describe the tragic scene:

"Her Majesty was unable to stand it long:
  She was overcome with grief,
  And when the Highlanders lowered the coffin
  Into the tomb she felt relief.
  The ceremony closed with singing
  Lead Kindly Light,
  Upon which the Queen withdrew in haste
  From the mournful sight."

Tennyson who was getting a butt of sack every year from the Queen as her laureate didn't tell us half as much about what was going on at Windsor as that. Incidentally this Leopold, M'Gonagall tells us, was well respected by everybody,

"Especially for his singing for the benefit of Esher School,
  Which proves he was a wise Prince
  And no conceited fool."

But you must not imagine that M'Gonagall was always in elegiac mood; at times he twanged a lyric lyre. Listen, for example, to his immortal "Invocation to the Cow." "The hen," this lovely pastoral begins, "is a noble animal

But the cow is much forlorner
      Standing in the rain
      With a leg at each corner."

That, I unhesitatingly declare, is the finest description of a cow in the English language. If you don't believe me just look out of the train the next time you are whizzing through Wilts or Lincolnshire. M'Gonagall was a great recorder of epic events, and nothing from the Zulu War or the Tay Bridge disaster to the opening of a branch railway line was too great or little for his melancholy muse. So when you are pledging the Immortal Memory of Robert Burns tomorrow night, my country-men, please spare a glass for that other Scottish bard, the Great M'Gonagall, who, poor, crazy creature that he was, tried, too, in his queer way, to keep the lamp of lyricism burning and when he died went out, as all his heroes did, "without delay and without dismay." The toast is M'Gonagall!

*January 24th,* 1947


## INS UCH ANIG

WHENEVER I am cornered by one of the surrealist suede shoes and polo pullover brigade and asked to animadvert upon some crazy green and gamboge concoction of twisted telephone receivers, skeleton mackerel, mammalian grand pianos on crimson icebergs, poached eggs squelching over red-hot roller skates, melting marzipan watches, negroid mermaids drinking tea from chinchilla teacups in seaweed-draped drawing rooms and pink waterfalls pouring upwards into a quicksilver sky flecked with black stars and Buchanan tartan clouds, I usually get out of it by murmuring that I am an industrial correspondent with leanings towards Mozart and Milton and that the masterpieces of Mr. Dali and Max Ernst are not for the likes of me.

So far this has worked reasonably well and I am seldom invited to surrealist soirées. But in view of last night's seance at the London Gallery in Brook Street I am wondering what on earth I can say to save myself next time I am cornered. For it seems that the Surrealists and the Dadaists—who reigned long before the Dali dynasty was founded—are coming back in a big way and are turning their queer contorted talents to the service of Thalia, the muse of lyric poetry. The surrealist Shakespeare apparently is an artist named Kurt Schwitters, who caused quite a stir a year or two back with an exhibition of "pictures" composed on odds and ends of rubbish and street garbage which, according to his devoted disciples, he "trans-muted by felicities of arrangement" into works of rare beauty.

This superb exercise in the higher realms of scavenging earned him an international reputation, but up till now outside the esoteric circles in which he moves Mr. Schwitters has hid his poetic light under a bushel. Last night in Brook Street, where Handel wrote "The Messiah," he recited some of his best pieces in what he calls "word deformations." Among his poems are "Furore of Sneezing," "Eve Blossoms Has Wheels," and a miniature masterpiece which he modestly calls "Small Poem for Stutterers." Take this exquisite lyric, for example:

> "LANKE TR GL
> PE PE PE PE PE
> OOKA OOKA OOKA OOKA
> LANKE TR GL
> PII PII PII PII PII."

That piece is in English, but later on Schwitters will give another recital to show he can write just as lucidly in German. As I rolled this lovely stanza over my tongue it occurred to me how much lovelier the famous "In such a night as this" scene between Lorenzo and Jessica would have been if only Shakespeare had known how to write in "word" deformations. Just listen to it!

> "INS UCH ANIG HTA
> STH ISWH ENT HES
> WEE TWIN DDID GEN
> TLYK ISS THET REES."

The more I think of it the more I am convinced that Mr. Schwitters is a poet of rare distinction and unique achievement, and when I am challenged by my Bloomsbury friends about him I shall say that and recite a piece of my own which I have written under his influence.

> "HONKE TONKE YON GAYA
> ICKY TICKY TOK TOK TOK
> YA YA YA YA YA
> WOGGA WAGGA WEE
> HA HA HA HA HA
> HAH."

I call that "Sunrise Over Senegal" or "Pennies For Bevin." It expresses the feelings of a little child eating ice cream covered with hot chocolate.

*March 6th,* 1947

# THE MAGIC OF WORDS OF ONE SYLLABLE

MANY and many a year ago, as Edgar Allan Poe, in his aery-faery way, wrote of that much more magical realm that floated so lovelily in the poppy fumes of his fantastic imagination, when I was a homespun loon in that far-off northern kingdom by the sea, there used to be a wandering and frequently intoxicated harlequin who came to see us every summer and make us merry with his drunken antics and quaint conceits. He was the principal clown in Pindar's Circus—a mammoth affair with at least ten horses, two elephants and a lackadaisical lion called Sirdar the Second—and he called himself Rossini the Great on the brilliant bills which showed him hanging by his teeth from a flying trapeze over what looked like the Grand Canyon, Colorado. We all knew his real name was Alec Ross, and that he came from Broughty Ferry, but we worshipped him for all that.

In the course of one amazing afternoon the great Rossini would stroll round the town on 20ft. stilts, cross the river on a high slack-wire, walk on his hands for half a mile along the river wall, drink a gallon of gasoline and then set a bonfire alight with his fiery breath, escape from a thing like the Iron Virgin of Nuremberg, dive in chains into the harbour, be pulled apart by the two elephants and finish up the day quite cheerfully with a brace of local blacksmiths with sledge-hammers smashing half a ton of free-stone on his bare head. And all the time, like one of the peripatetic philosophers in Plato's academy, he scattered words of wisdom as he went along in a high-pitched stream of hiccuppy sentences while he kept replenishing his mighty frame from an enormous flagon filled with what the Parliamentary correspondents call "an amber-coloured liquid" when the Chancellor has a dispatch box binge on it on Budget Day.

Now you are doubtless wondering why after all these years I have dragged the magnificent Rossini from the tomb where, I feel certain, even at this moment, his nimble bones properly pickled in the mountain dew are beating a brisk tattoo upon the coffin lid. Well, I have summoned him from the vasty deep—as he would have put it as he came up shimmering like a porpoise from the harbour bottom —because in his queer way he had the answer to a problem which has just been put to me by a young reader. Which, she asks, is the best way to write? In long, rich, flamboyant sentences like Conrad and Gibbon, or in short, crisp, clipped sentences like Hemingway and O. Henry?

Rossini used to pose this very problem as he swayed on his stilts over us all those years ago. "Once upon a time," he would croak, "there was a coloured individual whose name was Uncle Edward, and there was no capillary vegetation upon his cranium, which is the precise locality where that fleecy substance ought to luxuriate." Then he would giggle and wave his bottle up at the Manse and the swell mansions at the top of the town. "That's what the toffs say," he would say, and take another swig. "But, as for me—there once was a nigger and his name was Uncle Ned and there was no wool on the top of his head, the place where the wool ought to grow." With which piece of literary criticism he would fall on to the roof of the Town Hall and shout all over the town "To err is human, to forgive divine."

Maybe Rossini's advice is not what my young lady wants, but I don't think she will go far wrong if she takes it for all that. For did not Shakespeare himself, in what is perhaps the most enchanted passage in all literature, manage to conjure up the magic in words of one syllable. Just listen to it!

> *The moon shines bright—in such a night as this,*
> *When the sweet wind did gently kiss the trees,*
> *And they did make no noise—in such a night*
> *Troilus methinks mounted the Trojan walls,*
> *And sighed his soul toward the Grecian tents*
> *Where Cressid lay that night.*

There are 48 words in that passage, and only eight of them are of two syllables, and four of them are proper names. Yet what a silver symphony of moonlight and magic under the Venetian stars Shakespeare has made of those four dozen simple everyday words which your fishmonger uses half a dozen times every morning—only in a different order. So there you are, Miss Somerton. And if you accuse me of spurning Rossini's advice and using long words when short ones would do, may I remind you that it was Shakespeare too who made my countryman Macbeth wring his bloodstained hands in terror and exclaim that so far from ever being clean again they

> *. . . will rather*
> *The multitudinous seas incarnadine*
> *Making the green one red."*

Perhaps the best thing is to try a bit of both, like Shakespeare!

*May 6th,* 1947

## MAGGS MAKYTH MANNERS

IF from now onwards you should detect a mellower and more gentlemanly note creeping into these melancholy lucubrations of mine you must blame it all on Mr. Maggs. For if it hadn't been for Mr. Maggs I should have gone blundering on in my boorish way, spitting venom, splitting infinitives and generally committing all the solecisms in the social calendar like the low, vulgar fellow I am. As it is, I am now, like Hamlet, by way of becoming the glass of fashion and the mould of form, a kind of modern mixture of Sir Philip Sidney, Beau Brummell and Mr. Eden. And all because of Mr. Maggs! In fairness to him, however, I must make it clear at the start that Mr. Maggs is quite innocent in this act and completely unaware of the revolutionary influence he was exerting on my future as he sat in the big book-lined room in Chancery Lane yesterday afternoon looking for all the world like General Smuts.

Perhaps at this point I should explain that my Mr. Maggs is *the* Mr. Maggs. The world's leading bibliophile and manuscript hunter who shares the sylvan solitude of Berkeley Square with B.O.A.C., the Coal Board, the Chase National Bank, the Mayfair Club, the Ministry of Transport, the International Time Recording Company, the nightingale and the Herne Bay Electricity Supply Company, Ltd.

Now it just happened at lunch time yesterday that the famous book hound and myself had the same idea and turned up together at Hodgson's book mart, where they were selling off a choice collection of beautiful books belonging to someone who was somewhat sketchily alluded to on the catalogue cover as "An English Gentleman." All I can say is that, to judge by his literary tastes which ranged impressively from Homer to Havelock Ellis, he must have been a rare and refreshing gentleman. What lured me to Hodgson's sunflooded chambers was the news that among the "gentleman's" more esoteric treasures was a rare edition of James Joyce's "Ulysses," illustrated by Matisse, and a complete collection of the Nonesuch Poets. Maybe, I thought, it will be a poor day for Hodgson, and I may just manage to pick up a bargain or two. So, jingling my bawbees, I sauntered hopefully in just in time to see Maggs waggle his world-famous beard and send the bidding soaring skywards far beyond my poor plebeian reach.

Whilst I remained, the lowest price was just under £3 for three of the Nonesuch Dickens volumes, but for the most part the bidding was quite out of my class. I couldn't help remembering that it was Mr. Maggs who paid £22,000 for the Gutenberg Bible only the other day, who gave £15,000 for Napoleon's love letters to Marie Louise, and bought the Codex Sinaiticus from the Soviet Government for £100,000. So when it became clear that he was determined to sit me out I fled further up the lane to a second-hand shop more in keeping with my pocket if not with my desires. It was there I found a delicious Victorian book on etiquette which claimed to make a gentleman of me in twelve lessons. As it only cost a bob I snapped it up and retired to the cloistral calm of Lincoln's Inn to commence forthwith on my new career as the Blessington D'Orsay of Bouverie Street.

It was encouraging at the start to be told that " while high birth and good breeding are the privileges of the few the habits and manners of a gentleman may be acquired by all." It was even more reassuring to learn that only a *slight* acquaintance with art, music and literature are required in the best Society and that while a clean skin and perfectly kept nails are indispensable it is only when you want to become "a perfect gentleman" that "the aid of a Turkish bath is compulsory." After warning me never to ride to hounds "in patent leather boots," never to trample on a lady's train and invariably to wear a black waistcoat if I cannot find a white one the sartorial Socrates goes on to declare that "it would be extremely bad taste" on my part "to wear the Koh-i-Noor diamond as a tiepin." To say nothing of the shock it would be to the Queen. Above all I must never put my feet up on strange tables and if I should be unlucky enough to drop a piece of my host's best china I must on no account offer to pay for it or tell the Duke—as Mr. Tittlebat Titmouse did on a similar occasion— that I know a nice little place in Tottenham Court Road where he can replace it on the cheap.

Finally, I am implored when eating out not to "make violent dashes at the dishes as they go round," or to follow the food greedily with eager eyes as it appears. On my way back I looked in again at Hodgsons and sure enough the inexorable Mr. Maggs, looking more like Smuts than ever, was still tapping his pencil and orientating his beard as the bids flew like blackbirds nearer and nearer to the ceiling. And now I'll never know who got my "Ulysses."

*June 13th*, 1947

## STROLLING ALONE IN LONDON

A S I wandered, lonelier even than Wordsworth's cloud, through the weed-covered ruins around St. Paul's on Bank Holiday morning, the queer feeling gradually grew upon me that I was the last man left on earth—the sole survivor of some shattering cosmic crisis compared with which Mr. Attlee's trumpery troubles are little more than a typhoon in a thimble. The pure, smokeless holiday air was as clear as crystal, and as I watched the drifting thistledown and gossamer go glistening down the wind I felt just like the man in M. P. Shiel's mysterious but half-forgotten masterpiece, "The Purple Cloud," who comes back from the North Pole to find he is the only living thing left on the lifeless, paralysed planet.

Mile after mile I strolled along through the sleeping squares of Bloomsbury, the vast yards of Smithfield and the empty, echoing canyons of the City, where only a few hours earlier the bulls and bears and stags and bucketshop men were dancing their financial fandangos—or should it be contangos?—among the Rio Tintos and Antofagastas. All the way I never saw a living soul until I got round to Fetter Lane, where I came across a Filipino sailor sitting on a wall among the willow-herb stroking a tortoiseshell cat.

Putting the cat down, he asked me where he could get a drink of water, but as London is not organised to deal with such extravagant demands I couldn't tell him. So, after giving me a look which clearly indicated that a country which couldn't provide a thirsty sailor with a glass of water deserved to be on the rocks, he staggered off through the thistledown on his way back to Honolulu or Hoboken or wherever Filipino sailors go when they can't get a glass of water in London.

Incidentally, as I spent all Sunday indoors, that Filipino was the first man I had seen, apart from a policeman in Russell Square and a bundle of rags curled up in a doorway in Leather Lane, since Saturday night when I spotted Bertrand Russell—his reluctant lordship—standing at the corner of Charlotte Street on the very spot where the gunmen murdered Antiquis. The great philosopher had just been having a bite at Antoine's, and when I saw him he was standing rather forlornly in the rain with a couple of young disciples, working out in that remarkable mind of his the relative chances of getting a taxi in Oxford Street or Tottenham Court Road.

One of the great delights of walking in London when it is empty is that you can read the odd things on the walls and take down notes without being mobbed or taken for one of Strachey's snoopers. I never knew, for instance, until yesterday that the foundation stone of the Church Missionary Society Building in Salisbury Court was laid on September 5th, 1913, by H. H. Daudi Chwa, Kabaka of Uganda, that Simon Bolivar, the great South American liberator, laid his plans to rescue his people in a house in Grafton Street, just off the Tottenham Court Road, or that the great Lord Palmerston used to write poems to his corns when he went to Dowie's in Wigmore Street for his boots. But the notice I liked best of all yesterday was in a grocer's window in Charlotte Street next door to the Fitzroy Tavern—London's La Coupole—which stated quite simply: "Kittens Given Away. No Points."

*August 5th,* 1947

## THE REAL AUTOLYCUS

ACCORDING to Bernard Shaw—who himself admits that he lifted his characters from Dickens and his ideas from Samuel Butler—Shakespeare picked up most of his immortal sayings by eavesdropping on Elizabeth, listening at keyholes, loafing about Fleet Street taverns and jotting down in his little book all the pearls of wisdom and folly as they fell from the lips of the casual passers-by. In other words, if the Shavian theory is correct, the Swan of Avon, like his own Autolycus, was a snapper-up of unconsidered trifles, and the old lady who complained that "Hamlet" was full of quotations seems to have been right after all. Be that as it may, I am glad to report that so far as the Fleet Street taverns are concerned the eaves-dropping business is still in full swing.

It was Mrs. Leach, of Brixton, who brought the Bard back to my mind when I opened my mail yesterday. She writes to tell me of an extremely odd trifle she snapped up in her local on Budget night. Listening to the hazy alcoholic hum about the wedding, the weather, Dalton, the spivs and the spuds, the following fantastic utterance, she says "suddenly fell on my astonished ears." "By the way, Bill, I looked up the categorical imperative in the Oxford Dictionary and they say it is the inward bidding of the conscience as the ultimate moral directive." Just that and nothing more. Mrs. Leach, the fair Autolyca, took it down and cocked her shell-like ear to hear, if possible, what wild whimsy it was that had so strangely summoned the mighty spirit of Immanuel Kant from the Elysian Fields to the saloon bar of a Brixton boozer.

Alas, we shall never know, for when she heard the voice again it was declaring "what a shocking shame" it was that Tommy Lawton should have the pick of 14 houses in Nottingham while there is a waiting list of workers stretching from the Black Boy to the far end of Sherwood Forest. But it does remind me of some queer snatches I have picked up myself during my career as a professional eavesdropper.

There was, for instance, the superb satiny sequiny lady in the tea-shop at Leamington Spa who drowned the orchestra one day by saying, "Of course, my dear, if it hadn't been raining Uncle Robert would have turned up and then where would Campbell-Bannerman have been?" Echo and the 'cello answered "Where?" Then there was the languid young toff in the corridor of the Royal Scot at Crewe, who was saying as he passed my compartment: "Pater was quite amenable but the mater is being perfectly execrable." Mr. Bevin would have loved the drunken Seaforth I overheard one night on the Boulevard Montmartre say to his speechless camerado: "To hell wi' this, Alec. We must get organised."

My own favourite eavesdrop was on that wild night when London was ablaze and the fire-bombs were falling like confetti on the crumbling city. The Temple Church had just caved in, St. Bride's was blazing like a torch, glass was flying like snowflakes and the manhole covers were going up like tiddlywinks. Suddenly from a dark doorway I heard a woman say, "I wouldn't 'ave nuffink to do wiv 'er, Nell, she's always poking 'er bleedin' nose into everybody's business and 'er man's not in the union."

*November 20th*, 1947

## THE OUTCOME OF A DAFT DIALOGUE

ONE of Fleet Street's renowned reporters, a man of exquisite taste, polished wit and vast erudition, threw a curious challenge at me over the luncheon table yesterday. Taking a deep draught from his flagon of Montrachet, he looked at me over the mimosa, poked a fork-full of lobster under my nose and said: "I'll bet you a barrel of oysters that you can't work the words ' orchidaceous ' and ' ineluctable ' into your column tomorrow.'

"Done," said I vaingloriously, tossing off a tumbler of iced water and waving a slab of steamed cod back at him. "And we'll go down to Whitstable and broach a barrel of Chablis as well if you succeed," the prince of prose replied and returned to his lobster.

This daft dialogue arose from a remark by the renowned reporter to the effect that I have been letting the word "esoteric" get the better of me lately. Long, rare and obscure words, he argued, are all right in their way, especially if you are a downtrodden columnist with a set acreage to cover every day like an ox. But once you succumb to such strange enchanted words, you are lost. They lie about lazily in your mind like exotic odalisques—false colourful creatures—and if you let them get the better of you, you will finish up, like W. J. Turner, the most word-haunted poet of our time, who became so bewitched by the magic and mystery of strange names that at last he had to confess: "Chimborazo, Cotopaxi they had stolen my soul away." Before that, he had wondered why the Mexicans had named a mountain "Popo-catapetl" and the ancient Romans a green leaf "Oleander." (For that matter, I have often wondered why the English called a yellow flower a daffodil and the Scots a mountain Schiehallion.)

It was with such odd notions in my mind that I left the renowned reporter caressing his Camembert, and came out into the icy sunshine. The sun danced like diamonds on the greasy puddles and bubbled like champagne on the squashed cabbage leaves in Covent Garden. It poured into the dingy, dusty corners of the slatternly streets and washed in floods of quivering gold on the steps of Inigo Jones's church, where Eliza Doolittle met Higgins and Pickering for the first time.

I turned towards the Strand, met C. B. Cochran looking as nimble and rosy as the liveliest of his young ladies, passed the Bodega (where I once saw Henry Ainley, Harry Pollitt, the Rector of Stiffkey and the public hangman, all unbeknown to one another, having their pints in the days when they threw the gherkins and anchovies in with the beer). All this time I was wondering how to win that firkin without cheating. I even thought of calling the sunshine "orchidaceous" and Mr. Cochran "ineluctable," but that would be stretching things a bit.

In the end it was the late Baron Reuter who rolled out the barrel for me. I bought a paper and there, among the famines, floods and fires was a Reuter message from Sydney about a man who found orchids so irresistible that he stole £90 worth of them. He was so orchidaceous that these exotic glooms were as ineluctable to him as Van Goghs are to young ladies in Regent's Park and white whisky was to my granny. Well, there it is, renowned reporter. I'm prepared to waive the trip to Whitstable and settle for a dozen Colchesters and a glass of Chablis at Wheelers.

*January 20th*, 1948


# UNFILLETED WITCHES

ONCE upon a time long, long ago in the springtime of the century, when all the world was young, I went all the way from Wick to Bergen in my bare feet and came back triumphant with a boatload of Norwegian witches. Even now, nearly half a century later, I can see them glimmering ghostlike in the hold, as the sun comes up in memory in great spokes and splinters over the Sotra fiord. You will see as we proceed why I have started in this Grimm fashion. It happened in the unkempt days when, with my wild companions, we roamed the summer seas like scruffy schoolboy vikings and scoffed at law and order with the insolent assurance of foolish flaming youth. When the school was shut—and sometimes when it was open—we were off hotfoot to the rocks and rivers on some existentialist exploit or other in the course of which no stone was left unturned or avenue unexplored.

Of all our escapades none equalled witch-hunting. Only the worst boys ever got the chance to join, and had there been a Minister of Labour at the time, no doubt we should have been banned too.

There was in those days—and I hope still is—a superstition among fishermen that it was lucky to take a boy with them when they went off to the herring grounds. A red-head was the best. Looking back on it from the cynical standpoint of an industrial correspondent it was a profitable whimsy for the fishermen. We scrubbed and washed up in the galley for 6d. a cruise. I can see now what abject little wage slaves

66

we were. But at the time it was sheer stingo. I wouldn't have swopped ships with Vasco da Gama or even Noah himself.

It all came back to me yesterday as I browsed in the exciting columns of *The Board of Trade Journal.* Suddenly I saw them glimmering again. in a Ministry of Food message on Page 844. They were stuck away between a piece about Crude Teaseed Oil from Hong Kong and a paragraph about Biological Percolating Filters. There was no hint of witchcraft in the headline, which was like a page from Jack Solomons's order book. "Imports of Boxed Fresh White Fish" is what it said. It went on to list fish Jack may now import from Norway and Sweden when he is not worrying about Woodcock. He can buy brill, soles, turbot, halibut, hake, ray and skate wings, roes, cod and whiting to say nothing of "dogfish—skinned and headed."

I was passing on to a spicy bit about "refractory bricks" when the witches leapt at me. There they were between the dabs and the dogfish.

"Witches" it said, may be imported from Norway and Sweden "provided they are not filleted or under ¾lb." In the Oxford Dictionary they are called *pleuronectes cynoglossus*, but fishermen call them witches "because of their uncanny appearance." They are, it appears, "well known in Grimsby and Manchester." Ordinary people call them dabs, lemon soles or long flanks. Anyway, on behalf of that long-lost boy who watched the Arctic dawnlight flickering on their ancestresses so many years ago, I thank Mr. Strachey for letting them in again.

Alas, however, I must report a shocking lack of liaison between Strachey and his comrade Harold Wilson at the Board of Trade. For while witches can now come in free, under Import Control Order 292, broom-sticks are still banned.

*November 4th,* 1948


## CAMBRIDGE RHAPSODY

ONE of the advantages of taking your summer holidays in the middle of winter is that it gives you a reasonable chance of a spot of sunshine. To say nothing of the fact that you can find somewhere to sleep in solitude instead of sharing an attic—as I once did in Weston-super-Mare—with a Welsh revivalist, a tea-taster from Walsall, and a man who kept whistling "In a Monastery Garden."

This does not refer to the Society swallows who fly to the Riviera in September and come back in time to grouse about the Budget in April. There are not so many of these birds about nowadays. And such as there are can be found in the grill rooms of Dublin and the Bahamas —where the £ can still look the $ in the face—praising God for sirloins, Sir Waldron and Ivor Thomas.

Haggard and worn with the relentless pursuit of pleasure, the Bahamas brigade must be thoroughly sick of sunshine, weary of cloudless skies and sapphire seas, fed-up with fun and thankful for the periodic passage of Rita Hayworth with her latest swain, to take their minds off their own monotonous merriment. It is here at home that the winter summer holiday is such a refreshing joy. And it has taken me over fifty years to find it out. They owed me a week, and the notion of taking it before the year died came to me on Christmas Eve when a friend invited me down—or is it up—to Cambridge. So I spent the first part of the week wandering in the academic groves of Erasmus, Milton, Newton, Gray and Thackeray, and the second half prowling about the livelier if less learned backwaters of London.

Christmas at Cambridge was pure delight. I stayed at Girton in a lovely house filled with beautiful books which "Q.," Gilbert Murray and "the Shropshire Lad" had handled, and pianos in every room which have thrilled to the touch of Honegger, Kodály, Alban Berg and the great Vaughan Williams himself. There was such a deep restfulness about the place that it was hard to remember that only a short walk down the road Thomson first isolated the electron and Cockcroft split the atom.

The colleges were empty and there was such sweet peace and quiet in the courts and closes that it would not have surprised you to meet Erasmus on his walk in Queen's Meadow or to have come across Newton and Halley strolling in the Great Court of Trinity or, as Shaw has them in his play, anachronistically arguing with Charles II and Kneller. Incidentally, there is an odd relic of the Merry Monarch in the library at Trinity—"a calculus or gallstone taken from the entrails of a cobbler's wife at Bury St. Edmunds, which was broken in two to satisfy the curiosity of Charles II when at Newmarket."

Another piece of original research I did on Boxing Day revealed that one of the main exhibits in the "Invertebrate Department" of the Museum of Zoology was presented by a Miss E. C. Jelly. My brow is not too high, however, and I trust you will not put it down to Celtic

68

whimsy when I say I went to Emmanuel just because Swift tells us that Gulliver spent three years there. Nor, I hope, will you call me a Philistine if I tell you that after leaving Newton and Milton behind, I got just as big a thrill on Parker's Piece when I walked on the very turf where Hobbs and Hayward served their apprenticeship at the queen of games.

Finally, I am sure you will understand why my heart leapt as I passed a certain house in St. Barnabas Road. For my mother once lived there. And, though she was only the parlour-maid, she once served tea to Rupert Brooke. I hope she had some honey for him.

*January 5th,* 1949

## BUCKINGHAM PALACE WAS MADE A ZOO

THERE is an alcoholic convention in this country—it can scarcely be called a rule—that public-houses are never named after a dead monarch until the reign of his successor is over. This means that anybody who can get a licence tomorrow morning can call his pub the George the Fifth but not the Edward the Eighth. Come to think of it, however, I have never heard of a pub called George V in this country or even of an Edward the Seventh, though there are plenty of Alexandras about the place. And over in Paris they not only have an Edward the Seventh and a George Cinq but an Edward the Eighth *and* a Duke of Windsor as well. Which only goes to show that when it comes to honouring kings and dukes the republicans have us old-fashioned monarchists licked to a frazzle. Whatever the rule or the convention about pub names may be, however, I am hopeful that Edward the Eighth's brief tenure of the orb and sceptre—he was long enough on the job to get his head on the stamps but not on the pennies —will absolve me from a charge of lèse majesté if I tell a comic story about George V which has never been published before. It has to do with influenza, budgerigars, Arthur Greenwood, the Zoo, and the King's famous macaw which used to perch on the back of his armchair and squawk at Baldwin and Ramsay MacDonald.

Those of you who keep a parrot or even a couple of lovebirds will recall the wild scare which swept Europe twenty years ago when people were dying all over the place from a queer new kind of influenza which they caught from parrots and budgerigars. The doctors called it psittacosis or parrots' disease. It began in Berlin and spread to Devil's Island, where 200 convicts died of it, and to Hollywood where Sally Eilers and Alan Hale caught it from a parrot when filming "Sailor's Holiday." England's first victim was the Mayor of Ashton-under-Lyne—himself a doctor—who died after attending a psittacosis patient. Then people with parrots fell ill all over the country and after a dozen had died the matter was raised in the House of Commons. That is where Arthur Greenwood comes in. After the usual promise to give the problem his earnest consideration, Mr. Greenwood—then Minister of Health—decided that the only thing to do was to ban the import of parrots altogether, and along with them parrakeets, cockatoos, cockatiels, lories, lorikeets, caiques, lovebirds, budgerigars and macaws. And that is where King George the Fifth comes in.

The ban was imposed on May 20, 1930, and it raised an immediate storm. Every old lady in the land with a parrot or a pair of lovebirds wrote to Greenwood calling him a heartless monster; the usual inter-necine strife broke out in Harley Street among the experts; and there was a solemn deputation of bailies in bowler hats and square-toed boots from Glasgow which turned out to be the headquarters of the budgerigar industry—Budgerigaropolis, as you might say. Just as things were getting hot and Arthur was thinking of going into a monastery, word came that Lord—then Sir Clive—Wigram, the King's Private Secretary, wanted to see him on urgent business. So he heaved a sigh of relief, threw the parrots into their appropriate pigeon-holes, and rushed to greet the royal envoy. Alas, poor Arthur. Sir Clive came straight to the point. "It's about these parrots," he said. Greenwood gulped. "Yes," he asked faintly, "what about them?" Sir Clive told him. His Majesty, it seemed, was extremely disturbed about the ban as he had just purchased a mate for his famous macaw and it was already on its way from Brazil. Couldn't something be done about it? Mr. Greenwood was sympathetic but severe. An Order was an Order, he pointed out, and was actually issued in the King's name. In such matters nobody was above the law. Besides, he said, the Brazilian macaw might give his Majesty influenza, and where would we be then? Sir Clive was worried, but just as things looked grim Arthur had a brain-wave. "Do you think," he asked, "the King would object if I were to schedule him as a zoological gardens for the time being?" This puzzled Sir Clive, but Greenwood pointed out that there was a special reservation in the Order which permitted the import of parrots provided they were for zoological gardens under proper supervision. Sir Clive looked a wee bit dubious, but said he would put this fantastic proposition to his Majesty at once. So back to Buckingham Palace he went to ask the King if he was prepared to be scheduled as a zoo. The crowd in the Mall probably thought he was bringing a message from Hoover or an ultimatum from Mussolini. Less than an hour later the King himself was on the phone to Greenwood. He pretended to be annoyed but was obviously intensely amused by the whole thing and impressed by Arthur's diplomatic device for overcoming the difficulty.

"What's all this damn nonsense about turning me into a zoo?" he demanded gruffly, but Greenwood could hear the chuckle behind the growl. Things were coming to a pretty pass, his Majesty went on, when even the King couldn't call his home his own. "Zoological gardens, indeed," he muttered.

Arthur was tactful, and explained the whole position to him as clearly as possible, and in the end the King chortled and said if he could only get a mate for his macaw he was quite willing that Buckingham Palace should be scheduled officially as a zoological gardens or even as an annexe of Transport House as long as the ban lasted. He wanted the whole transaction kept dark, however, as he didn't want to have crowds coming to the Palace "and a fellow on the gate taking tickets from people wanting to see the wild animals." And so it was done. Buckingham Palace became a "zoo," the King got his way, Greenwood got away with it, the macaw got his mate, and so far as I know the palace is officially scheduled as a zoological gardens to this day. Looking back on it all now nobody is quite sure if the parrots were to blame for the disease after all and only thirteen people seem to have died of it. Arthur, happily, is still with us collecting pennies to beat Woolton's pounds. But I wonder what'd become of the macaws?

*October 13th, 1949*

## CONSIDERED TRIFLES—ON A NO. 15 BUS

WHEN G. K. Chesterton called one of his best books "Tremendous Trifles" he was not just showing the world that he was the prince of paradox-mongers and high priest of organised chaos who loved to stand on his head to make the rest of the world look wrong side up. He really did believe, not only that trifles were tremendous but that tremendous things, like his own gigantic carcase, were mostly trifles.

G.K.C., however, was no mere snapper-up of unconsidered trifles like Autolycus, though, like that immortal and melodious spiv, he did believe and prove in a prodigious cataract of sparkling verse and blithe, pugnacious prose that a merry heart goes all the way. All Chesterton's trifles were considered ones, no matter whether they were tiny or tremendous, and that is why I think he would have been happy if he could have left Don Quixote and Dickens in the shades for an hour or so yesterday afternoon and travelled with me from Marble Arch to Fleet Street in a Number 15 bus.

The morning, which began with brilliant splendour in a frosty flush of sparkling champagne sunshine which danced and glittered on the plate-glass windows, proved to be as false as it was fair and most of us waiting for the bus outside Selfridge's were late, wet, cold and peevish. As I never wear a hat and, like the mysterious man in Sonnet 34, had travelled forth without my cloak I was soon as soaked as a water spaniel and my smart American shoes—which I bought in Washington last year when a radiator burned a hole in my good stout English ones—suddenly began to leak. And to top it all the red dye in the cover of "Martin Chuzzlewit," which I am reading at the moment, began to run until I must have looked like Macbeth or Buck Ruxton with my "hangman's hands."

To make things worse I had to write this column before six o'clock and I hadn't one idea in my head. Which only goes to show what happens, even to a garrulous old gossip like me, when he goes on a pub crawl like the one we have just finished.

It was then that the first trifle came to cheer me up. When the conductress asked for my fare at Oxford Circus I just said "Fleet Street, please," and she punched a $2\frac{1}{2}d.$ ticket and went away humming "Confidentially." I hadn't the heart to call her back and tell her I got on half a mile back, so I decided to cheat the London Transport out of $1\frac{1}{2}d.$ and turned to Betsy Prig. Then at the Café Royal I looked up and saw a ravishing young strawberry blonde sheltering in the doorway with a beige bulldog that looked for all the world like A. V. Alexander trying to look like Churchill. She caught my admiring eye through the streaming window of the bus and just as we began to slide away towards Piccadilly Circus and out of her life—I suppose for ever—I'll swear she smiled at me.

By this time life was beginning to look a little rosier and before Mighty Joe Young, the monstrous gorilla with the electric eyes above the Monico, could make me shiver again, there was my sweetheart Myrna Loy smiling at me beneath the hooves of a red pony from the façade of the Plaza, and Orson Welles glowering at me from a Viennese sewer on the front of the Carlton.

Then as we swung round into Trafalgar Square, where the fountains were flashing back at the rain and the workmen were getting Nelson ready for his annual jamboree, I am sure I saw Mrs. Braddock sailing up the Strand like Congreve's Millamant with all her pennants flying. Not that I would suggest for a moment that the redoubtable Mrs. Braddock is in any way a trifle; and if that determined lady I saw sweeping past the Corner House like an avenging angel was not Mrs. Braddock I hereby apologise to them both for looking so remarkably like each other, and, may I add, so brisk and bonny in the rain.

Mrs. Braddock or whoever it was cheered me up no end and when I saw a man coming out of a shop opposite the Tivoli wearing a pith helmet I wanted to get out and do a rumba with him. I expect he was one of Dick Plummer's groundnuts men trying out his new kit. At Aldwych, which I never pass without recalling the night the bomb fell in front of the Gaiety with me cowering in the doorway of Inveresk House—where Winston brought out the *British Gazette* during the General Strike—I thought there was a fire. But it was only the crowd around the Aldwych Theatre looking at the pictures of Bonar Colleano beating up Vivien Leigh and Renee Asherson in "A Streetcar Named Desire."

When I thought of the old carefree days of the Aldwych farces when Ralph Lynn, Robertson Hare and Tom Walls were always losing their trousers, I wondered what the world was coming to. And, incidentally —being a Scot—I marvelled at the incomprehensible English who fill half the West End theatres and cinemas with American smash hits just at the very time we need every dollar we can beg, borrow or steal. For when you come to think of it all that Margot Fonteyn and Moira Shearer are doing in New York is dancing themselves almost to death to earn dollars to pay Danny Kaye and Harpo Marx.

But by this time I was in Fleet Street and I got down among the

73

divorcees and the bankrupts outside the Law Courts and went off to buy myself a pair of shoes. And then, dry-shod, I strode past Dr. Johnson in the ruins of St. Clement Danes and had a mild and bitter in the Rainbow where Belloc and Chesterton used to talk about such trifles in the age of gold. Then when I came out I ran into my ancient crony Con O'Leary, the most Irish Irishman that ever lived and a writer who learned the trade from the leprechauns. A broth of a boy indeed.

There was still one trifle left to cheer me up, however. Outside St. Dunstan where his comrades of the craft had just been remembering Robert Lynd I saw a sign which told me a thing I never knew before —that MacDonald the Rector is also the Rural Dean of the City of London. No wonder Izaak Walton worshipped there. Finally, as I came through the Temple I noticed, as I do every day, that Oliver Goldsmith's grave is still missing. Will no one tell us where it is? And so in my new shoes and much merrier than when I set forth from Selfridge's I got to my desk at last to find somebody had sent me a new pen with which I sat down and wrote this.

Trifling, I call it.

*October 21st, 1949*

## READING ABOUT YOUR DEATH

IT was characteristic of Mr. Churchill—who is nothing if not original in these matters—that when he heard the other day that he was dead he did not deny it point blank or follow Mark Twain's well-worn example and say the report was greatly exaggerated. He was wilier than that. He just made a mild remonstrance that he was still very much alive and left us all wondering who could have started such a stupid rumour. It has done nobody any harm, least of all the "corpse," who appears to be livelier than ever. What interests me most about it, however, is that it has placed Winston beside his old Parliamentary colleagues Arthur Greenwood and Jennie Lee in that select gallery of great ones who have read about their own deaths. Nearly every day somewhere or other somebody has to deny that he is dead. But for some reason so far as I can discover from the records

Churchill, Greenwood and Jennie are the only living politicians who have been, as you might say, prematurely posthumised.

I often wonder why the "living dead" don't form a club. There would be no shortage of members. Bernard Shaw—thrice "dead"—could be the president and Vesta Tilley—twice "dead"—the mistress of ceremonies. And if, in spite of G. B. S. and Vesta, the club were ever short of entertainment, it could call on Bing Crosby, Danny Kaye and Louis Armstrong, the trumpeter, who has met Gabriel at the Pearly Gates no fewer than five times according to the newspapers, but is still tootling away on Broadway as if he were really alive. They ordered these things better in the old days. Look at Lord Brougham, my distinguished but disgruntled countryman, who gave his name to a carriage and his money to the sharks at Nice and Monte Carlo. He decided to "die" just to see what the world thought of him. So he sent the news of his death to the papers and waited to see the result. It was not so pleasant at first, but he had the laugh on the House of Lords later in the day when he walked in and heard them chortling over his demise.

In our own time there was Jimmy Thomas. I remember the first time he "died." He came into Annie's Bar in the old House of Commons chuckling like a cherub. There were only Joe Devlin and myself there at the time, except for old Ned Scrymgeour, the Prohibitionist, who was having a glass of distilled water and a cream cracker in a corner. We nearly fainted when Jimmy, who was not notoriously open-handed—cried: "What'll you have boys? I'm dead!" One of the evening papers had just "killed" him. He lived another 25 years after that, but whenever I met him—even once in Geneva— we always had "one on the corpse." Then there was Tim Sandell of Camberwell Green, who was reported dead three times and is I believe the only man ever to attend his own inquest outside the pages of Mesdames Christie and Sayers. I was not there when it happened, but I'm told that Dr. Cowburn the coroner looked exactly as Macbeth did when Banquo turned up at the banquet. As one of the Baker Street Irregulars, I must not forget Sherlock Holmes, who was so foully "murdered" by his own creator. But he connived at it himself so I suppose he doesn't count.

Looking through the records I find some queer fish among the famous folk who have lived to read their own obituary notices. Apart from Mark Twain, who obviously loved it, there are King Edward (three times), Queen Victoria (once), Squire Bancroft, Augustine Birrell, Sir Robert Ball, the astronomer, John Burns, Lloyd George, Lord Lascelles, Jennie Lee, Poincaré, Hindenburg and Joffre. Then there was Lottie Collins, who used to sing "Ta-ra-ra-boom-de-ay" in the naughty 'nineties. On the night she was reported dead she came on kicking higher than ever crying, "There's life in the old dog yet." Of all the premature dead, however, my favourite is Mr. Kudo Kumekawa, of Kobe, who was reported dead in 1906. He admitted it in a graceful letter to the editor and invited all his friends and the editor to his funeral. They made a real banzai binge of it, and Kumekawa, in a white shroud, walked in front of his coffin to his grave. And when they got there he threw the editor in and sprinkled him with ink. Finally, I was once posted "missing" myself in the Kaiser's war and sometimes wonder even now if they found the same fellow.

*February 22nd, 1950*


## NO BONES ABOUT IT

CONSIDERING how rarely anybody thinks a new thought or does an original thing nowadays, it seems a pity that Signor Ubaldo Ubaldi got so little space in the newspapers when he died in Bologna the other day. For he was a man of ideas who discovered a new way of disposing of his body when he was dead. Even in these days of newsprint famine I should have thought that papers which devote whole columns to Denis Compton's knee could spare more than a four-line paragraph to the whole of Signor Ubaldi's bones. The signor was a notable criminal in that ancient seat of learning and he has just died after a distinguished career dedicated to Proudhon's sound proposition that all property is theft. He was Bologna's principal burglar and it is a sad commentary on the state to which that ancient calling has fallen that he left only £12. And that, if you please, in the city where Benvenuto Cellini once got away in one night, not only with the local count's gold and jewels but with the countess as well.

If that £12 had been all Ubaldi left he would not have been worth a paragraph except perhaps in the local paper on which his fellow cracksman Mussolini was once a reporter. But Ubaldi was no mere

Bill Sikes. He had a soul above jemmies and life-preservers and each night as he sallied forth to relieve the Bolognese bourgeoisie of their surplus value he sang "Santa Lucia" to himself, and when he came home with the swag he would put on his carpet slippers and play "Caro Nome" on his clarinet. He loved music so much, indeed, that he could hardly bear the thought that when he died he would not be able to take his clarinet with him. He brooded on this a great deal and then hit on the novel idea of turning himself into a clarinet when he was dead. So he left, along with the £12, an instruction to his executors that his bones should be polished and made into clarinet mouthpieces.

This seems to me a very sensible and charming idea. Surely in these days of controls and visas, when nobody can call his soul his own, it is a comforting thought that we can still do what we like with our bones when we are dead. After all, the human body is not so important as all that when the spark of life has gone. Scientists tell us that for practical purposes the ingredients in an average man's body are worth just about five shillings, which compares very unfavourably with that of a pig or a sheep. Even Stalin, it seems, is 90 per cent water and there was not enough iron in Bismarck to make a tenpenny nail. There is hardly enough lime in Joe Louis to whitewash a chicken run or carbon in Bernard Shaw to make one pencil. And if you took all the materials which made up Alexander the Great, Napoleon and Hitler you would not get enough sulphur to make a box of matches. Maybe that's what Hamlet meant when he said that Imperious Cæsar "dead and turned to clay might stop a hole to keep the wind away." Though I would not go as far as the late Lord Knutsford, who said that all bodies should be dissected or thrown into the sea, I am all for people doing what they like with their own corpses.

Old Jeremy Bentham—who can still be seen sitting in his evening dress in the University College Hospital—wanted everybody to be embalmed and be his own statue. It has been reported many times that my friend Datas, the memory man, has already sold his head. Though I am not a morbid man, I sometimes wonder what I should do with my remains when the time comes. At one time I thought I would have my ashes scattered among the spruce trees on Morven, my boyhood mountain, but then the awful thought occurred to me that I might come back to Fleet Street some day as a roll of newsprint. Then I toyed with the idea of having my ashes secretly poured into the pepper-pots at the Carlton Club, but that, I thought, might put some ginger into them. In the end, probably, I shall follow Signor Ubaldi's example and have my bones made into bagpipes. Like most Highlandmen I am a big-boned chap and they should make several sets of drones and chanters out of me. I can think of no better way than that of having my revenge on this cruel world. So if one night towards the close of the century you hear a pibroch sounding in Piccadilly don't pass by without dropping a coin in the piper's tam o' shanter. He may be playing me.

*October 21st,* 1950

## ON THE LEVEL

MANY years ago when I was an industrial correspondent and moved imperiously about the globe like a trade union leader, I founded, along with my old comrades George Thomas of the *Daily Herald* and the Marquis of Donegall a secret society which, I regret to say, never fulfilled the roseate promise of its auspicious birth. We formed it one golden morning over a flagon of raspberry brandy beside the Fountain of Elephants in Chambery. And we made the Marquis our first president, not on snobbish grounds, but because he is the Lord High Admiral of Lough Neagh, the largest sheet of pure drinking water in the United Kingdom.

Despite our exalted patronage there was nothing highfalutin about our society. It had no lofty purpose. We were not out to convert anybody, to raise money for anything, to rescue the perishing, or even to regenerate mankind. So far as we were concerned mankind could stew in its own juice. Uplift was the last thing in our minds. *Au contraire*—that's the *Chambery fraise* still talking after all these years—we were, quite literally, levellers. We had just one aim—the flattening out of Switzerland. Since then Mr. Thomas, who is an extremist in these matters, has sought to saddle the society with new objectives, such as levelling the surface of the Atlantic and making the sun rise and set at the same time everywhere. These are admirable aspirations, but we must not be diverted from our original goal. First things first! It will be time enough to mess about with the Zodiac when the Matterhorn has been put in its place level with Lac Leman and the Rhone laps the summit of Mont Blanc.

78

Meanwhile, before we turn our attention to the Atlantic, there is Sir Clive Morrison-Bell to be dealt with. Sir Clive was once secretary to Lord Roberts and is still, in his eightieth year, an active member of the Alpine Club. I hate to think what he will say when he hears about our society. Even the modest proposal to run a railway up the Matterhorn has roused his sleeping fires. In *The Times* yesterday he protested against what he described as "this sordid project" and said "there is something revolting about a railway up the Matterhorn." Why is there something "revolting" about a railway that goes up the Matterhorn and not about one that runs through Holland? What's wrong anyway with riding up a mountain in comfort if you feel like it? So far as I am concerned mountains are things to look at. I am willing to walk all over Switzerland on the level, but when it comes to what Dr. Johnson would call perpendicular perambulation give me the funicular every time.

If I had my way there would be a railway up every hill more than 50 feet high. Personally I have no desire to look down on my fellow men. In these matters I am not a steeplechaser. I find all the fun I want on the flat. But why should the enjoyment—if such it is—of these mountains be confined to a few bold spirits with the time and courage to climb them? There are millions who would love to go up the Matterhorn but cannot face the cruel climb. Nobody wants to stop people going up the hard way if they prefer it, but surely, if science can make it easy for them, the old crocks have as good a right as the human goats to get to the top. But you must not think the funicular is the final answer. Nothing short of complete flattening until the whole place is like the Sahara will do. A start should be made at once. Switzerland has for too long been a land fit only for heroes to live in.

*June 21st, 1951*

# HAUNTED BY HOLMES

THOSE of you, if such there be, who have followed these rambling meditations of mine for any length of time, will have noticed by now that I keep returning, again and again, to Shakespeare, Shaw and Sherlock Holmes. Now and then, it is true, I make a passing reference to such rare spirits as Socrates, Pascal and the Great

M'Gonagall, but for the most part I have been faithful, in my Autolycan fashion, to the Bard, the Sage and the Sleuth. This is not surprising. I have been pilfering from them for so long that I would find it hard to live without them. For the newspaper columnist can no more get rid of Shakespeare, Shaw and Sherlock than the Ancient Mariner could shake off the albatross or Mr. Dick could forget King Charles' head.

There is Holmes, for instance. He has been haunting me this week-end.

First of all he has been condemned once more as a capitalist hack by the Soviet arbiters who decide such things. And Mr. Maurice Richardson reminded us in *The Observer* that twenty years ago, before Stalin sponged him out, the great Radek said it was not an accident that "the efflorescence of Sherlock Holmes coincided with the apogee of British Imperialism."

This is very much like saying that the rise of Danny Kaye coincided with the fall of Hitler, or that when it's night-time in Italy it's Wednesday over here. It confirms the view I have long held that the Soviet leaders have given up Marx long ago and are now following Mrs. Nickleby.

Then there was my old crony Lionel Hale who, in the Round Britain Quiz on Sunday, put forward the astonishing theory that Holmes was the original Abominable Snowman. All the evidence he can produce for this, I fancy, is that Holmes, disguised as the Norwegian explorer Sigerson, was in Tibet about the time the Snowman's footprints were first seen. This is pretty thin. For by the same reasoning you could prove that Dr. Johnson was the original Loch Ness Monster as he was in Drumnadrochit a day or two before it was first seen in 1773.

On top of all this comes Mr. K. C. Hart, of St. Leonards-on-Sea, who has written me a letter in which he accuses Dr. Watson of double dealing.

Mr. Hart has been doing a bit of sleuthing on his own and has discovered that 18 paragraphs at the beginning of The Resident Patient and The Cardboard Box are exactly the same word for word. The only difference is that in the first story it was "a close rainy day in October," while in the other it was "a blazing hot day in August." In each story "Holmes lay curled upon the sofa reading and re-reading a letter which he had received by the morning post." In each "the morning paper was uninteresting, Parliament had risen and everybody was out of town." And in each Watson "yearned for the glades of the New Forest."

This is the famous thought-reading passage where Holmes astonishes Watson by telling him what he is thinking merely by watching him looking at pictures of General Gordon and Henry Ward Beecher. Mr. Hart thinks Conan Doyle was cheating and wonders how much he made out of it at five shillings a word. The answer is that he made nothing though he did, in a way, cheat.

What happened was that when the Memoirs of Sherlock Holmes were published there was no room for The Cardboard Box and the whole thought-reading sequence was transferred to the Resident Patient. And so for many years the two stories went round the world with the same eighteen paragraphs in them. When, however, the collected edition of the short stories was published years later, the passage was restored to The Cardboard Box where it rightly belongs. But Doyle made nothing out of the duplication as the words in question were sold only once to the Strand Magazine.

In any case I am not inclined to blame Conan Doyle—or Watson for that matter—too much for this, as it is one of the most enjoyable passages in the whole of the Sherlock saga. After all, if his friend Elgar could go on for nearly an hour with his variations on one theme surely we should not be too hard on Conan Doyle for repeating himself just this once.

Let us therefore forgive him and hope that nobody will go into it any further in the hope of proving from it that Holmes after all was Watson. That, as Henry James would have said, would be going too exquisitely far.

*March 4th*, 1952

## WITH RICHARD II IN THE TRAIN

IT was pure coincidence that I should have been reading "Richard the Second" as the Royal Scot, like a sleek sinuous cat, went purring through Lancaster on Sunday afternoon. The famous train was very late and it looked as if we would be lucky to reach London on the right side of midnight. For some reason we had been pottering about in the lovely vales between the Lakes and the Pennines and stopping in the middle of lonely heaths where new-clipped sheep looked on at us, as we drank our wine and iced water, as much as to say: "What have these poor people done to be cooped up in a hot clanking prison on such a day?"

I was on my way back to London from Languedoc by way of Aberdeen. This Chestertonian proceeding was due to a date I had with Eric Linklater and Robert Boothby in the old bailiwick of Banff. I missed the night train from Aberdeen and had to motor to Glasgow to catch the Royal Scot in the morning. Which explains why I was reading Shakespeare in Cumberland when I should have been basking in my garden in Hampstead. It was odd that I should have reached old John of Gaunt's famous speech about the sceptred isle just as I was going through his home town. But how apt it was on such a glorious day.

England has never looked lovelier than she did on Sunday as we huffed and puffed from Carlisle to Crewe. Even the dark Satanic mills seemed to fit into "this blessed plot," and the ragamuffins plunging into the woodland pools and oily canals looked like the real offspring of "this happy breed of men." It was a day of wild and lovely irrelevance as if Mrs. Nickleby herself were on the footplate. We pulled up in the midst of cool woods, among herds of dappled cows beside tumbling rivers filled with shouting children, between the eyeless walls of gasworks, in the shadow of vast slagheaps, on bridges overhanging market towns and on the Ship Canal where a big steamer sailed through the farmlands with the cattle looking in at the portholes.

The colours of Cumberland were beyond all description. It was as if Cezanne and van Gogh had done the land and Monet and Turner the sky. Vast fields of daisies like great iced cakes and lush meadows glowing with buttercups were suddenly splashed with lilac and almond blossom and foaming gushers of moonlight-coloured may.

Here and there a bank of Canterbury-bells shimmered like blue smoke among the silver birches which looked like glistening bones and when we got up on Shap Fell "the golden broom did blow." In one big daisy field a herd of jet-black cattle browsed, looking for all the world like a convocation of Calvinists and near Thrimby Grange, miles from anywhere, a lonely man in a bowler hat was patiently cleaning an engine called "Palestine" with a crimson cloth.

Near Oxenholme, where the sky was full of larks, an old tramp was making his meal on a stick fire. He looked up as we crawled by and I'm sure he was enjoying his tin of smoky tea far more than I was my glass of Medoc. High over Carnforth a hawk hovered and I fancy he could look down on the decks of ships far out on the Irish Sea. There was too much loveliness to last and when we got to Preston the clouds were boiling up for a storm. Somewhere near there I heard a cuckoo calling and I dozed off with Old John of Gaunt on my knee. When I woke with a jerk I saw the words: "Uncle Joe's Mint Balls Keep You All Aglow," and I knew we were in Wigan.

By now all the colours had drained out of earth and sky, and as we spanked along through the drab lands I realised what Belloc meant when he said the Midlands are "sodden and unkind." As the shadows fell and the lightning flashed I was reminded that this world of ours, beautiful and full of fantasies as it is, is only a ball of mud and metals floating in a field of deadly forces. And that we are as helpless as Wordsworth's Lucy who "rolled round in earth's diurnal course with rocks and stones and trees."

But as old Gaunt said, "small showers last long, but sudden storms are short." And by the time we rattled into London the sky was clear and the night filled with the friendly odours of the town. And when I got to Hampstead there was my own familiar owl to hoot me home. For even if Cumberland was full of Wordsworth's cuckoo's progeny I can hear, when the wind is right, the great-great-great-great-grandson of Keats's nightingale whistling to Coleridge's same old moon.

*May 20th,* 1952

## LOST HOUSES CAN NEVER BE FOUND

THOSE of you who are old enough to remember that almost forgotten genius Stacy Aumonier may recall that one of his most delightful tales was called Where Was Wych Street? It was—indeed it still is—a most amusing story about the witnesses in a law suit who could not remember, only a few years after its demolition, where one of London's best-known streets used to be. The street in question had been pulled down to make way for the majestic thoroughfare we now call Kingsway and all the old familiar little bookshops, taverns and shaving saloons where the witnesses had browsed, caroused and gossiped for so many years, were obliterated by the heavy load of commercial, scholastic and theatrical masonry which gives that part of London such a queer antiseptic look of colourless dignity. The point of the story was that, though they had all spent the best part of their working lives passing up and down the lost street, they could not agree as to where it was before it was knocked down.

I am reminded of this old problem by one of the L.C.C. Press officers, who has written to me explaining why there is no plaque on the house where Mahatma Gandhi lived in Store Street. Nobody knows where the house was. There is no doubt he did live in Store Street, for I have read letters from him dated from there. But owing to the combined operations of Hermann Goering and the Senate of London University, substantial stretches of that street are now covered with stately temples of the arts and sciences.

When I first came to London I lived in a hut called after Shakespeare at the corner of Store Street, and from my window I could watch the swallows skimming among the chimney pots of Torrington Square, where the lofty beacon of London University now stands. It was somewhere beneath that educational Everest of cement and steel that Gandhi lived at the turn of the century, and dreamed of Swaraj and the day when he would establish his bloodless empire over the mind and soul of three hundred million people. Nobody will ever find it now. Like Wych Street it has passed away into the gloom of forgotten things, and soon there will be nobody left to remember it has ever been.

I had the same sad feeling of the mutability of sticks and stones the other day when I could not find the house—or even the street—where Milton was born. It has all been blown away and there is not even a hole in the ground to remind us that a few yards from St. Paul's, in Broad Street, the loftiest spirit—if not the greatest genius—that England ever produced came into the world in the house of a humble scrivener who amused himself, when the ledgers were laid aside, in writing madrigals. Even the desk on which this is written occupies a bit of space where Walter Scott's hard-done-by hero, Nigel Oliphant, hid when he was in the toils of Lord Dalgarno and Dame Suddlechop. But who could tell now, save for the name of Hanging Sword Alley, where Jerry Cruncher, the body-snatcher, lived, that such dreadful things went on where Cardinal Shy and Mr. Cummings now contemplate the passing show in their peculiar fashions.

The tragedy is we don't remember for very long. Soon we think only of the things that happened in those lost corners and not of the places themselves. For the greatest of all paradoxes is that the voracious cormorant Time gobbles up the real solid things, the sticks and stones, and leaves only the fantasies and dreams to go on for ever. The towns where Homer smote his "blooming lyre" are crumbled and forgotten, but men still read, with awe and wonder, about what happened to Ulysses and Nausicaa, who never existed at all.

Who can remember who was Prime Minister when Gray wrote the Elegy or when Pickwick met Sam Weller? I have no doubt Mr. Denis Brogan could tell you. But if Dr. Gallup puts the question to the first 500 people he meets in Kingsway I will bet him a new calculating machine that they can no more answer it than they can tell him where Wych Street was fifty years ago. What a pity it is that Charles Lamb when he was at it did not write a sequel to his poignant poem and call it "All, all are gone, the old familiar places!"

*September 6th*, 1952


## THE GOING OF SMOKY JOE

THERE is, I am sure, no political significance in the fact that National Cat Week this year straddles the Labour and Conservative conferences. For whatever else she may be, the ordinary common or garden domestic tabby is not a partisan. All cats, in fact, are cross benchers. There used to be a black cat at the Winter Gardens, Blackpool, which would stroll on to the platform during Labour, Liberal, Tory or Communist conferences with contemptuous impartiality. Once, indeed, I saw Lord Woolton almost burst himself with delight when this magnificent mouser strolled on to the platform while Mr. Churchill was speaking. I hadn't the heart to tell him that only a few days before the same fickle feline walked into the middle of one of Mr. Morrison's perorations. There are, of course, cynical people who allege that the whole thing is arranged by Woolton and Morgan Phillips standing in the wings waving a kipper to lure Tabitha into the limelight.

There is a sense, however, in which all cats are Conservative, the Socialist ideal means nothing to them and even Liberalism has little attraction for them when they are in search of their prey. There are still thousands of Manx cats in the world, but who has ever heard of a Marx cat? They share, it is true, the belief in the materialist conception of history and in London at any rate they are very much alive to the surplus value of the hotel refuse bins. But they are not collectivists. Like Kipling's cat, they all walk by themselves, the extreme isolationists of the animal kingdom.

During the coming week strenuous efforts will no doubt be made by cat lovers to raise the living standards of the cat world, and thousands of lonely spinsters who have nothing but their tabbies to share the changes and chances of the world with them will lavish a little more than their usual love on them. But there will be little or no communal celebrations by the cats themselves. Most cats, when they are not on the tiles, are about as fraternal as Mr. Deakin when he greets brother Bevan in public. They are incorruptible individualists, unlike dogs, who are friendly and fond of the fellowship not only of human beings but of other dogs as well.

I have never had a dog, but last year I was honoured with a visit by a strange cat which I christened Smoky Joe and took into the house as one of the family. He was a friendly little chap and for several weeks he purred and played about the house creating indescribable chaos among the wool and knitting needles. He settled down in his basket in the kitchen between the sink and the ironing board. Before long he had made a major revolution in the economy of the household and then just when we had turned our lives upside down to make him feel at home he vanished as mysteriously as he came. People who have experience of both tell me that a dog would never have done a thing like that.

The purpose of the Cat Week, I am told, is "to draw attention to the fact that cats and kittens are the most neglected of all domestic pets." That may be so, but I can't help feeling that they bring most of it on themselves by their superior attitude of Olympian aloofness. The most bellicose dog has a strong affection for his master and even Bill Sikes, who gave him little else but kicks, was loved by his bulldog. There are many stories of dogs being broken-hearted on the death of their masters, like Greyfriars Bobby, the famous Edinburgh dog who refused to leave his owner's grave until he died of grief and starvation. But who has ever heard of a cat dying of grief or even noticing that his mistress has died so long as the saucer of milk and the piece of fish is still there?

Personally I am not a cat man or a dog man. So far as animals are concerned I see no reason to be a Morrisonite or a Bevanite. On the whole, I think I would prefer a cat as it knows how to look after itself better than a dog, like the cats in the Roman Forum who have survived since Caesar's time apparently without a bite of food or a drop of water. But I am bound to say that though I got to love Smoky Joe very much I am not anxious to fill his place and his basket is now used as a depository for spanners and clothes pegs. The cat is an aristocrat and a snob; the dog a democrat and a mixer. Even the most miserable cat —and it is for them more than anything that I hope the Cat Week will be a great success—is not as miserable as a rule as its master.

No doubt they have their trials like the rest of us, and to judge by the amount of pills and powders I had to buy for Smoky Joe during his brief sojourn beneath my roof, they have their stomach troubles as well. But they seem to have about them even at the worst of times that inner serenity which Aneurin Bevan told us at Morecambe is the essential condition of a full and happy life. At all events, next week should be a happy time for cats as well as Conservatives. And if Lord Woolton arranges, as usual, for a black Persian to stroll on while Mr. Churchill is speaking, I hope the delegates will give it a good reception.

Whatever happens I hope nobody will be cruel to his cat or walk it off its feet, as Dick Whittington did to his poor companion. For even if they are snobs, cats are not vindictive and if they do get away with an occasional piece of fish or brisket that was not intended for them they are inhabitants of the same planet as ourselves. And, as Burns said to the mouse:

> *A daimen-icker in a thrave*
> *'S a sma' request.*

My grandmother, who shared Cleopatra's belief that there will be cats in Heaven, may be right after all. Who knows but that the cat purring away there in front of the fire, may get there before me? And if that should be so it will surely be better for me to get a good report from him than a bad one. I am not suggesting that Paradise will be parcelled out to us according to our deserts, or that we can buy a corner of it by bribing the cat. But a bigger saucer of milk or an extra bloater or two may help.

*October 6th,* 1952

# PART FOUR

# Diverse Encounters

## THE LAST OF THE REBELS

IT was, I think, that scintillating infidel Voltaire who declared, in answer to one of his devout detractors, that even if there was no God it would be necessary, for all kinds of social, political and philosophical reasons, to invent him. The same thing, in a minor and more mundane degree, may be said about that remarkable old rebel who died in Dublin yesterday, all but forgotten by the modern world but loaded with legends and the love of his fellow-men. For if ever there was a character whose appearance on the scene was vital, necessary and inevitable it was Black Jim Larkin. He was—after Tom Mann and Ben Tillett had gone—the last of the old revolutionary guard and with him dies away—let us hope for ever—the last faint rumblings of the barricades.

Though he was still—as far as can be ascertained—two years short of the Scriptural span, Larkin was really the last romantic relic of an angry turbulent age when ordinary decent men and women were often compelled to resort to riot and revolt to redress wrongs and to establish simple rights and privileges which were denied them by reason. Today I doubt very much whether Larkin would have made such a noise in the world as he did when he first came storming into the headlines out of the stinking slums of Liverpool. Though he was by no means just the wild mob orator and demagogue that the Tories made him out to be—there was too much heart and soul in him for that—he was always more at home on the soap-box than in the Senate chamber.

Perhaps the best way to sum him up is to say that he was to the industrial side of the Labour movement what Maxton was on the political front. Like the great Clydeside agitator, he had a tremendous dynamic appeal combined with a lovable personality which made even his bitterest enemies—and the world was full of them—proud to be linked with him. And if life led Larkin along a rougher road and into tighter corners than Maxton had to contend with, they were striving after the same noble goal. They were both quenchless idealists with the same fierce flame burning inside them which nothing, prison, poverty, persecution, neglect, misrepresentation, disease and death itself could put out. In fact the more the Larkins and the Maxtons were persecuted the fiercer grew the flame inside them until it became a blaze which warmed a whole generation of poor men and women and lit lamps in dark places which will never be extinguished.

For many years Jim Larkin was the "voice" of inarticulate Ireland, the man who put into warm, living, pulsating phrases the thoughts and dreams of the great Labour leader, James Connolly, whose early death in the Easter Rebellion was, in my view at least, probably the heaviest hammer-blow that poor Ireland has ever suffered. I only once had the luck to see him in action and then he was old and tired, but I remember how he mounted the rostrum with his head high and shoulders squared as if he were a boxer leaping into the ring.

At times he let his emotions play havoc with his reason, as on the fantastic occasion of his return from Moscow where the Comintern had elected him to a Committee of 25 strong men who were going, said Jim, "to take over the government of the entire globe." And to lend an air of verisimilitude to this particularly unconvincing narrative he went on to assure the bold boys that a Russian army was on the march to back up the Irish workers and that the Soviet Fleet would be in the Liffey in a jiffy.

He was always inclined to be a bit fanciful when he took to party politics, and it is as a great strike leader that he will be remembered. He was with the Communists for a few years, but that wild soul was never meant to move in predestinate grooves. So nobody was surprised when the party chucked him out for what the *Daily Worker* quaintly described as "renegacy." Perhaps the greatest moment of his tempestuous life was that Sunday morning in 1913 when he eluded the contemporary Gestapo of Dublin Castle and appeared in the midst of the military at a meeting in O'Connell Street—we called it Sackville then—which had been proscribed by the British Government.

My colleague William Duckworth was there when it happened. O'Connell Street was packed and there was no sign of Larkin, who had declared the day before that no matter what the British did he would turn up on the stroke of eleven. Duckworth was in the lounge of the Imperial Hotel as the hour approached, and still no Larkin.

Then just as the clock began to boom eleven an ancient patriarch who had been reading the Sunday paper opposite Duckworth leapt to his feet, dashed out on the balcony, whipped off his whiskers and cried in a voice that could be heard in Wicklow: "Comrades, here I am. Jim Larkin, as I promised." What matters it that he spent that night in Mountjoy Gaol. That was the real Larkin that will live as long as there's a drop left in the Liffey.

*January* 31*st*, 1947

## HURRAH FOR THE PRINCIPLE

HE was quite the most miserable man I have ever met; a kind of melancholy amalgam of Mrs. Gummidge, Dismal Jimmy, Deirdre of the Sorrows and the wax Arab who hangs on a hook over a slow fire in Madame Tussaud's. The sort of fellow who takes his goloshes with him to the Riviera, wears a belt as well as braces, carries a coat *and* umbrella, walks under ladders for fear of being run over in the gutter, and wishes you a "Merry Christmas" in hollow, dismal tones as if he were singing "The Diver." To him, one feels, there is a dark cloud to every silver lining and every dawn, however rosy, is but the prelude to another sunset. Had he been evacuated during the blitz to Staffa or Benbecula, I feel sure he would have begun his new life among "the tangle o' the isles" by building himself a deep shelter at the bottom of Fingal's Cave.

I came across him first in a second-hand bookshop just off Holborn. He was shuffling about in the gloom at the back of the shop when I came in, and after a minute or two he fixed me with a wan and watery eye and asked if I did not think it was high time that something was done to put a stop to public processions and foolish wasteful ceremony when the Government was urging everybody to work harder, faster and longer. He didn't put it quite as lucidly as that, but I took his point and, in the best Scots style, answered his question by putting another. What, I asked, did he propose to do about it? This seemed to stump him for, like many another social revolutionary, he was much better at diagnosing diseases than at dealing with them. He urged me not to misunderstand him. He was not against public demonstrations when there was some definite social, economic or military purpose behind them, and he had nothing against the King. But, he went on, stooping sadly towards me like Atlas, as if all the weight of the world's woes were on his seedy shoulders, surely something should be done to keep the streets clear, so that those who did want to work could go about it without having to fight like football fans or travel ten miles round the Inner Circle to get from one side of Fleet Street to the other. Didn't I think it a bit thick that he had to hang about in Holborn for over an hour when he ought to be in the Temple with his lawyers?

I tried to console him by saying that his lawyers were probably drowning their grief at his absence in the forensic corner of the Clachan. So far from cheering him up this seemed to deepen his gloom, for he wobbled his Adam's apple a bit and said, "That's just it. Absenteeism, that's what it is, aided and abetted by the Government and dignified by the presence of the King, and, mind you," he added lugubriously, "the Tories and the Liberals are no better than the Socialists when it comes to this kind of tomfoolery." When I tried to argue that it wouldn't make an ounce of difference to the national effort if Molly takes a few minutes off to cheer the King, that Cripps won't lose a ton of exports if Maisie stands on a lamp-post to say, "Oh, my, ain't she lovely," or Milly goes out for a moment to pick up a few ideas from Princess Margaret's hat, and that it won't cost Dalton a single dollar if Mr. Cummings or the Editor of *The Times* is caught in the crush, he just sighed and muttered mournfully that it's the principle of these things that matters. And then he said with a sepulchral sob, there was all that sand and spit and polish, to say nothing of the shocking waste of big, strong policemen who would be better employed tracking down murderers and gunmen and collaring white-slave traffickers. At this stage I did not think it worth while to point out that the spit and polish would have been done anyway, that we have had very few gunmen or murderers in the City for quite a while, that the white-slave traffic East of Temple Bar is monopolised by news editors, and that if there is one thing Old Mother England has never been short of, even under the Strachey-Shinwell terror, it is sand.

In any case just at that moment a mighty roar from the Strand told us that the Royal Family was going by, and that their foolish subjects in open defiance of the *Daily Worker* were actually cheering them. So the miserable man, as Dickens would have called him, went on his funereal way to the Temple, the shop-girl still chewing strenuously away, with Socrates and Shakespeare looking sagely down at her pretty head dived deeper into her book, and after buying a midget volume telling me "How To Behave Like a Lady," I called in on my apothecary and consumed a beaker of bismuth and returned to my desk to tell you how I watched the King go by.

*May 16th*, 1947

## DAINTY DAISY WAS PHANTOM OF DELIGHT

THOSE of us who have had the rare joy of knowing and loving that remarkable woman, not only in the gay flamboyant spring-time of her astonishing triumphs, but in "the lonesome latter years" as well, will find it hard from now on to remember that Dainty Daisy Dormer is really dead. She was such a vibrant little imp of mischief, melody and loveliness that I came to look on her as part of the eternal scheme of things, and long after she had vanished from the limelight glare I kept coming across her, and all the time she seemed to grow younger and younger.

She always reminded me of that lovely whimsical double star Algol, which keeps going in and out at irregular intervals, but always comes back fresh and bright and sparkling just when you think it has gone for ever. Just when you thought you had lost track of her she would turn up on Brixton Hill in a beautiful club where real fish swam round you as you danced, or in Bloomsbury, where she was the charming hostess in a cosy little tavern which she filled with Persian kittens and portraits of all the stars she had scintillated with from Dan Leno down to the brothers Flip and Flop, who had just arrived in town. And then one grey morning she vanished again and I was sick at heart until one blessed day when I called at a wayside inn at Godalming and found my radiant goddess presiding over the provincial pint pots with all the gaiety and grace with which she had once held the whole wide world in thrall.

I first fell in love with her one wild wet night in Liverpool way back in the Kaiser's war when I climbed clammily up into the "gods" at the old Olympia to see Wilkie Bard. Mr. Bard was missing for some

93

reason and we all booed and blew razzberries until *she* came floating on like an angel out of paradise.

She came shyly from the wings swinging her sunbonnet and looking so wistful and forlorn in the savage glare of the limes that I wanted to shout "shame" at the big fat manager. And then she smiled at me, I'll swear, and sang "Don't You Remember California in September," and all the bells of heaven went ringing in my ears. We cheered and cheered and clapped and clapped and she came back and gave us "The Roses Round the Door" and "Goodnight, Mr. Brown. I'm Out." But it was no good. We whistled and stamped and yelled until she came back once more and sang "Back Home in Tennessee" and finally—what we had all been longing for—that immortal classic, "I Wouldn't Leave My Little Wooden Hut For You."

But it all had to end and the wicked curtains closed on that beauteous vision for the last time and I crawled disconsolately back to barracks feeling very much as Bottom the Weaver must have felt when the dream was ended and the real world closed in on him once more. You must remember that I was young and full of dreams. I had caught a glimpse of glory as that sweet girl sang that night. How much more glorious I should have been in my chill cot that night could I have seen that the day would come when I should know and love a dear old gracious lady in a Tottenham Court Road tavern who sometimes, on cold winter nights, would pull up to the fire and croon "California" to her tumbling colony of cats.

*September 16th*, 1947

## THREE MERRY MEN GO TO PARADISE

NOT since that far-off April morning way back in 1616 when the creators of Falstaff and Sancho Panza turned up together at the pearly gates has there been such rejoicing in the Elysian Fields as there must have been last week when those divine drolls and first-magnitude stars Will Fyffe, George Mozart and George Carney went twinkling into Paradise hand in hand.

If ever three mortal men were on the side of the angels they were the boys. Already, I feel sure, they are babbling in green fields with Sir John and browsing in the glades of asphodil with Sancho, Yorick and Bottom the weaver, and all the other immortal wags who have purified the earth with the great gales of their mirth. Though, like the slapstick clowns in scarlet wigs, they made their living out of laughter, they were not just comics.

In their way they were all iconoclasts with a clean, crisp philosophy to expound. They were far from prim or puritanical and could cuddle a wench or drain a flagon with the best. But they had nothing in common with those boisterous and salacious bores with concertina trousers, elastic-sided boots and Bardolphian noses burning in the middle of their pasty Pagliacci faces, who leer lecherously in the limes at bevies of beefy young women with starchy solidified smiles and knobbly knees.

Of the three I knew Mozart best. He was a queer little marmoset of a man with merry eyes and twinkling feet, and when I used to meet him in later years in his pub near the Coliseum I was always half afraid he would run up my arm, perch on my shoulder and nibble maraschino cherries, of which he was curiously fond. The Mozartian magic was as simple and as difficult to explain as a minuet by his immortal namesake. He used no wigs, props or make-up, yet in the twinkling of an eye he could change from a peppery Poona brigadier to a West End johnny ogling the girls and a sweet simpering young thing taking tea with the vicar.

In many ways Carney was the most polished comedian of our time and it has always puzzled me that he never got to the top. Some say he offended the V.I.P.s by his poignant study of the ex-officer in his ragged British warm picking up fag ends in the Mall as the strains of a string band playing the "Blue Danube" floated softly from the warm windows of Buckingham Palace. Be that as it may, he made the stalls wince every night, for those were the days when the Tories were balancing the Budget on the bellies of the unemployed. Carney did also a lovely sunny sketch of an Italian hokey-pokey man, but it was that down-and-out officer that haunted the halls during those years.

Will Fyffe, too, was an acute social critic, though not so bitter as Carney. That only made his lash bite deeper. I do believe his famous boozy ballad of Glasgow Town is as human and ironic as "Tam o' Shanter," if not quite so well written, and will probably last as long.

I am sure Falstaff and Sancho, Dan Leno, Jack Pleasants and Harry Weldon—aye, and Aristophanes—were there to welcome them in.

*December 16th,* 1947

## NO RATS, NO HASHISH

DOVER.

AFTER three weeks of compulsory clean living and high thinking on the snowy slopes of one of the better-class Alps it was somewhat shattering to my self-esteem to find myself confronted at Dover with a Treasury proclamation warning me of the dire fate that would befall me if I tried to smuggle any musk rats into the United Kingdom. In view of the fact that for 21 days—apart from a night at the Bal Tabarin—I had been conducting myself consistently on the moral and social principles of the pig-headed young man in Longfellow's exceedingly cold poem, I was very indignant. I asked my companions with a certain amount of acerbity if I looked like a musk rat smuggler. Neither, I proudly proclaimed to the crowded Customs House, was I a snuff smuggler, a hashish runner or a peddler of Indian hemp. Warming to it, I heatedly disclaimed all connection with benzolmorphine, coca leaves, bay rhum, opium, encodol plumage and plate, or any of the other odd things on Dr. Dalton's list, and protested loudly that I had never even when I was a child harboured any desire to bring cats, canine animals or parrots into the country. All I had was a pair of nylons, a Swiss watch, a two-way stretch and a hot-water bottle that was made in Birmingham and found its way to Zurich as part of Cripps's export drive. Young Beatty with the green chalk let me get by with that lot, and I just managed to scrape on to the Golden Arrow as it moved off for Victoria. But—and this is the point of dragging this all up again—many of my fellow-travellers didn't get through in time, and though every seat in that train had been booked up weeks before there were several empty seats. Protests are pouring in from stranded and delayed travellers, and the Southern Railway— quite justly, I think—is putting all the blame on the Customs people. In the old days there were enough men on the Customs counter to clear a full boat in about 15 minutes, but nowadays many people hang about for an hour. This sort of thing doesn't happen on the French side, where the brigands do their dirty work on the train. When the great day arrives when Mr. Bevin buys his ticket at Victoria and goes "where the hell he likes," I hope he will go the whole hog and kick the Customs counter out of his way as well.

*September 17th, 1946*

# THE IMPORTANCE OF BEING ERNEST

### BLACKPOOL.

WHEN Hamlet told Horatio that there were more things in Heaven and earth than were dreamt of in his philosophy it is highly improbable that he had Blackpool in his mind or that he was looking forward from "the dark backward and abysm of time" to the 1949 conference of the Labour Party. Yet I feel sure that if his melancholy nibs had looked in at the Winter Gardens here this morning when Ernie Bevin was having his annual romp round the universe, he would have turned to his abject stooge and said: "I told you so, Horatio."

For who, outside the Snake Pit, would have forecast even a year ago that the day would come when Bevin would stand up before a Labour Party conference, speak for 40 minutes in tense silence and sit down 'midst thunderous applause with 1,500 delirious delegates on their feet cheering and hip-hooraying with wild enthusiasm?

It was only two years ago at Margate that Ernie—more in the rôle of Cæsar that time—accused the comrades of stabbing him in the back, and three years ago at Bournemouth the police were so busy keeping an eye on him that for a time they missed Neville Heath, who was sitting meekly in the same hotel quietly contemplating his next exploit.

This morning I watched Bevin at work from the top gallery among the chandeliers, and it was astonishing to see the amazing magic of the man working its spell over the enormous audience. Taking his speech, sentence by sentence, there was nothing very new or sensational about it. It was a quiet, sober statesman-like review of his work during the past four years, and as such it was frank, comprehensive, justifiable, unusually clear, concise and modest, and overwhelmingly convincing, even if he did manage—perhaps naturally—to forget all about Palestine and the Ruhr.

In a way it was a flat, featureless speech devoid of drama or dialectical fireworks until the final cryptic passage where he mourned that age must take its toll. But it had us all on our feet at the end. Now the odd thing about it is that nobody knows how Ernie does it. I have been following him round England and Europe for over a quarter of a century, but I still cannot define the strange hypnotic power he has over the rank and file. There is something mysterious—even Mosaic about it. When he speaks you feel you are in the presence of a major prophet and though his notes are few, sketchy and squiggly he holds them and reads them as if they were the tablets of the law.

Keir Hardie had this strange gift. Ben Tillett had it. Lloyd George had it. Oddly enough Churchill and Morrison haven't got it. Their spells are of another kind.

When Bevin finished this morning the delegates were almost dancing with delight, and a Swedish pressman turned to me obviously puzzled and asked what it was all about. He had followed every word Bevin said and could not see any reason for the enthusiasm. I could not explain it to him, for though I, too, was a bit under the spell, I didn't understand it either. Cynics, of course, say it is all bluff and blarney and part of Ernie's act. This won't do, however, because all my colleagues at the Press table who have been listening to Bevin as long as I have agree that there is some strange magnetism about this extraordinary man.

They tell me the magic doesn't work in the House of Commons. Maybe this is because, as he revealed in his speech today, Ernie doesn't understand the House, and always has to ask Morrison what to do next.

Whatever the reason for his power, there is no doubt it exists. Two years ago when the crypto fellow-travellers, pacifists, Zionists, Arabs and the "Keep Left" brigade were all against him, Bevin had a rough run every time he got up to speak. Today most of them have melted away like Sennacherib's army and when he sat down *everyone* rose to him.

*June 10th*, 1949

## REMEMBERING ABBEY POTTERSON

JUST as seven cities claimed to be the birthplace of Homer as soon as he was dead—"through which the living Homer begged his bread"—and there are several places on the Italian Riviera where Columbus was born, so there are at least half a dozen hostelries on the London waterfront which claim to be the original tavern Dickens had in mind when he described the "Six Jolly Fellowship-Porters" in "Our Mutual Friend."

It is a fascinating, if profitless, pursuit to try *and* map out these countries of the mind. And I am sure if "Boz" came back today he would laugh at the devoted Dickensians who point to the very house where Pickwick lived, the iron bollard on which the Artful Dodger used to lean, the corner where Silas Wegg had his stall and the shadowy staircase in the Temple where Magwitch came out of the past to knock Pip's life sideways. Just as Conan Doyle would laugh at the hordes of schoolboys and Americans who scour Baker Street every summer looking for 221b where Holmes and Watson stayed but never notice the real houses where Pitt and Mrs. Siddons used to live.

We are all guilty of snooping after shadows, I am afraid, and of every hundred who can trace Pickwick's travels almost yard by yard there isn't more than one who could tell you who was Prime Minister at the time or even who was on the throne. It was no wonder therefore, that when Christopher Morley, the Bone brothers, H. M. Tomlinson, Grover Higgins and I landed at Limehouse Causeway from the police pinnace Patrick Colquhoun we made a bee-line for the Grapes Tavern which has as good a claim as any to have been Abbey Potterson's pub. Dickens, you may recall, describes the Six Jolly Fellowship-Porters as "a tavern of dropsical appearance, long settled down into a state of hale infirmity." In its whole constitution, he went on, "it had not a straight floor or hardly a straight line, but it had outlasted and clearly would yet outlast many a sprucer public-house." Inside the sawdust bar, where Rogue Riderhood used to scowl at the inspector and Bob Gliddery, the pot-boy, made eyes at Lizzie Hexam, there were "corpulent little casks, lemons in nets and biscuits in baskets." Dickens's prophecy has come true. The old inn has outlasted many a stouter building, survived the blitz and seen even Chinatown pass away into the gloom of forgotten things.

Today, nearly a century later, the place is pretty much the same except that genial Bill Higgins and his cheery spouse preside over Miss Potterson's counter and the march of progress has done away with the biscuits and lemons. The odd thing was that with a boatload of Dickensians like Morley and Tomlinson, the Bones and Grover Higgins—he had a special pint with his namesake on the veranda— nobody could remember Abbey Potterson's name. It was only after the landlord had searched his archives under the counter and un- earthed a letter from an octogenarian in Vancouver that we found out. How fortunate it was we had forgotten old Abbey Potterson. Otherwise this astonishing letter might have lain there beneath the mild and bitter for another century.

The letter came during the blitz from Mrs. Emily Ferris, of 811, East 45th Avenue, Vancouver. She was 84 then. When she was five her father took her to the Grapes, where Dickens used to sit in the big room upstairs and where Mrs. Higgins now has her spotless kitchen. But it was in another house opposite, the Barley Mow, that Abbey Potterson worked. Her real name was Mary Ferguson, says Mrs. Ferris, and Dickens just lifted her bodily across the road and placed her behind the bar of the Six Jolly Fellowship-Porters.

In those days Mrs. Ferris's aunt, Emily Judge, was the "serving maid" at the Grapes and there is a painting by Napier Henry with her in it. She says that Dickens frequently came to see his godfather, Christopher Huffam, who sold oars, masts and ship's gear round the corner in Church Row. Mrs. Ferris's grandfather was a close friend of Mary Ferguson, whom Dickens turned into Abbey Potterson, but she thinks the Six Jolly Fellowship-Porters may have had bits of the Two Brewers at the corner of Duke Shore in it as well. Tomlinson, who was born a mile or so away in Poplar and has just re-read "Our Mutual Friend," was intensely interested in all this. "What a man Dickens must have been," he said. "There must have been a demon in him."

From Dickens we crossed the river to greet the wraiths of Whistler and Rossetti at the Angel, Rotherhithe. It was on the veranda here that Whistler painted some of his loveliest nocturnes, which my sour countryman Ruskin described as "a pot of paint flung in the public's face." Alphonse Legros and Monet came here, too. James Bone told us a grand story about Alphonse. When he became a naturalised Englishman Monet or somebody asked him what on earth good it would do him. "Well, you see," replied Alphonse, "from now on I can always say we won the battle of Waterloo."

Then we went up river to Cardinal's Cap Alley on Bankside. We got to it through thousands of cases of French vermouth. Shakespeare surely walked along this narrow lane and it was almost certainly Dr. Jekyll's hidey-hole whenever he wanted to change into Mr. Hyde. But great Shakespearian and Dickensian though he is, I fancy that Chris Morley was disappointed that nobody could show him the old wharf down Deptford way where Sherlock Holmes chased the Andaman Islander in "The Sign of Four" with the poisoned arrows

whistling round his ears. For Chris is one of the founders of the
Baker Street Irregulars, the famous club of American Holmes fans.

As we said good-bye at Blackfriars I said it was good to see the river
so busy. "It had better be," said Tomlinson, "for when it stops being
busy London will die."

*October 7th,* 1949


# THE ANGRIEST MAN I KNEW

ON Sunday night as I listened to Kingsley Martin's exhilarating
broadcast about his old crony H. G. Wells it was astonishing to
recall that little more than three years ago I used to pass the time of
day with that vivid old man in the Chestnut Walk in Regent's Park
and come across him feeding the ducks or gossiping with the newsboys
outside Baker Street Station. So close could you get to genius in those
days.

There was one magical morning I remember when I saw Wells and
Bertrand Russell saluting each other outside Gog's Wine Lodge while
Cecil Day Lewis and Stephen Spender stalked past on the other side
of the street like the shape of things to come. It made me feel as
Davies, the tramp poet, must have done that morning when he heard
the cuckoo and saw the rainbow at the same time. "A rainbow and
a cuckoo's song may never come together again—may never come
this side the tomb."

Then as Martin and Frank Horrabin went on discussing Wells
I began to feel older still, like the man that Browning asked, "And did
you once see Shelley plain?" And it occurred to me that if I can survive
the peace conferences and arms agreements of the next two or three
decades I may very well pass the twilight of my days in the corner of
some village inn yammering away among the yokels about the great
days when I spoke with Shaw and Wells, drank beer with Belloc and
Chesterton, wine with Arnold Bennett, pernod with Liam O'Flaherty,
porter with Con O'Leary and tea with Galsworthy and Henry Handel
Richardson.

Kingsley Martin's summing-up of Wells could hardly have been
bettered, though I was a little disappointed that he did not make more
of the short stories and bring out more clearly the wild, divine, white-

hot anger of the man. I have a private notion that God, in His infinite wisdom, sends at least one angry man into the world in each generation to sweep the souls of men clean and keep us all from going to sleep. They are the bellmen of eternity who summon mankind to the march. And there has never been an angrier man than Wells. When confronted with poverty, pettiness, cruelty, injustice, muddle and above all stupidity he could be as savage as Swift, Voltaire and Aristophanes combined.

Sometimes a fortunate generation gets two angry men at the same time like Savonarola and Luther, Voltaire and Rousseau, Dickens and Balzac, Ibsen and Nietzsche, Whitman and Dostoevsky. In my young days Britain was blessed with at least three fierce spirits with flashing swords who were always sallying forth to slay dragons—often of their own creation—and exalt the soul of man. Whenever again will there be such a trinity of intellectual fomenters as Shaw, Wells and Chesterton, with Belloc always sniping from the wings?

It was of them chiefly that Kingsley Martin reminded me. As I listened to him describing the gorgeous rows that raged between Wells and Shaw in the old Fabian days my mind went back to a wild night in the Kingsway Hall when G.B.S. and Chesterton debated Socialism with Belloc in the Chair and people like Wells, Bennett, Huxley and Galsworthy scattered about in the hall. The crowd rushed the hall not to howl them down but to hear them, and the crush was so great in the end that if Shaw had not hauled me up from the Press table to the platform I should have been squeezed to pulp.

There were meetings like that all over the town in those days. They were the days of free thought. Tonight I doubt if you would find a first-class debate going on anywhere if you were to search every hall and schoolroom between Aberystwyth and Aberdeen. Some people blame the B.B.C. for this, but I blame the big political parties. In the old days men and women were encouraged to be intellectually adventurous. Today they have to toe the party line.

In a way it was a great pity that Wells and Shaw came along when they did, but I suppose it was inevitable. No two men anywhere in the world, certainly in our time, have had so much influence on the minds of men as they have had. And of the two—though he was not so big or sweeping as Shaw intellectually—Wells was the stronger force. For only the other day in Italy I came across two school kids in Milan with their eyes glued to a sensationally illustrated translation of "The Sleeper Awakes." They will probably never hear of Shaw.

They tell me that nobody reads Wells nowadays. I hope Kingsley Martin has put that right. For Wells was in many ways not only the angriest but the wisest man of his time. It is very queer to think that he ended his days chatting away garrulously to the girl in the bookstall in Baker Street. I don't think she ever knew who he was. It's a rum go, as Mr. Polly would say.

*December 20th*, 1949

## CHAMPION BORE IN A TAM O'SHANTER

IF ever there was any doubt in my mind that the Scotch bore is the worst of all bores it was dispelled yesterday, once and for all, when I shared a seat in a bus for more than three miles with the biggest bore I have ever had to suffer even in my 30 years in Fleet Street, which, as all the world knows, is the principal habitat of the species.

There was one superb Fleet Street bore before the war who used to clear the street whenever he emerged from his dismal den in one of the northern suburbs. He spread a trail of terror in the taverns between St. Paul's and Temple Bar, and even abandoned dipsomaniacs went on the water wagon and concealed themselves in shadowy coffee shops when he was about. When he died—it was said he bored himself to death—the industrial correspondents danced in the streets. He was what you might call a born avoidee. Until yesterday, when that Scotsman walked into the bus in Praed Street, I never thought I should look upon his like again. But compared with this new chap he was a flashing wit worthy to exchange sallies with G. B. S. and Oscar Wilde.

Let me tell you about the man from Tranent. He joined the bus at Paddington and left it at the Law Courts. That means we had him with us for nearly four miles and more than half an hour, every minute of which was as long and miserable as a month of Scottish Sundays. It was a cold wet morning and we were all huddled up in our winter woollies with our noses stuck in our books and papers when he swept in on us like an icy blast from the summit of Schiehallion. You could feel the air congeal as he swung himself on board. After informing the conductress, who was fairly blue with the cold in spite of her woollen helmet and mittens, that it was "a cold morrnin' " he made straight for the front seat and squelched himself in beside a poor pallid little woman with a wet boa round her neck and what looked like a cabbage strainer in a string bag on her lap. He was wearing a Rob Roy tam o'shanter and a Macleod muffler; and his big blubbery face, covered with a thick veil of purple veins, looked just like the harvest moon coming up on a winter night over the moor of Rannoch.

After a power of puffing and wallowing he removed his muffler and tam o'shanter and imparted to us all in a whisky croak the astonishing news that he came from Scotland. He pronounced it Skoatland, and added with a queer leer that he was not ashamed of it and didn't care who knew it. Then he fixed his glittering eye on me. There was only the gangway between us, and it was useless to bury my face in my book. I might as well have tried to stop Niagara with that woman's cabbage-strainer. Leaning over me he asked point-blank with a whiff of whisky and braised onions if I did not think Scotland a grand place to come from. This was when I made my big mistake. We were at the Marble Arch. I should have got out and dived into the Underground or the Serpentine. Instead, I tried to be witty. There was, I said, no better place in the world to come from than Scotland. In fact, I myself came from there as fast and as soon as I could. Alas! Your Scottish bore has an impregnable armour against that kind of thing. He has a mind like a waterlogged sporran enclosed in a mash of oatmeal and cockie-leekie. He was as pleased as Punch. "Now I'm richt gled tae hear it," he replied, and asked me if I kennt Tranent?

What could I say to that. I knew vaguely that there is a third-rate football team in Tranent and that Lord Beaverbrook's parents lived there before they went to New Brunswick to bring that mercurial moonbeam-chaser into the world. So I mumbled something about Beaverbrook. That meant nothing to him. Tranent, it appears, is the foremost civilised community on the face of the earth and the people there "the finest God"—he called him Goad—"ever put breath in." To this I replied that it seemed a pity he ever had to leave it. Once again the shaft went harmlessly past his flaming head and he said simply, "Aye, life is like that. But mind ye, I intend tae settle doon there in Tranent when I retire." Then he told me all about his old boyhood chums in Tranent and said he kept in touch through the Co-op. He gave the figures for the last divi and said it was one of the most go-ahead Co-op shops in the country. That would break poor Beaverbrook's heart.

And so it went on all down the Strand until he got up at the Law Courts and said he hoped we would meet again some morning to finish "a grand crack." The last I saw of him was a flash of tartan as he disappeared up the entry on the way to the School of Economics. And my mind went back to my old Fleet Street friend who has lost his place in my mind as the biggest bore in all the bleak realm of boredom.

*November 9th*, 1950

# THAT BED TOOK ME BACK

MANY years ago when there were still a few "characters" left in Fleet Street, I knew a man who worked all night—like Balzac—in a little room in Ludgate Circus and slept all day in a fantastic bed in Clapham. His name was Churchill and he claimed, without enthusiasm, to be a distant relative of the statesman whose politics he deplored, Winston being a Liberal and my friend a Tory at the time. His job was to follow the movements of steamers on *Lloyd's Shipping List* and to see they were transmitted over a private wire to a Plymouth newspaper with speed and accuracy. He did this with great efficiency and in time he taught me to do it too. There he would sit all through the night in his cosy little map-lined room high above the sleeping city, following from tropic to tropic and shore to shore the great ships as they steamed up and down the waterways of the world. From Hammerfest to Hobart one way and Shanghai to San Francisco the other, he watched over their landfalls and departures, shepherded them through tempests and typhoons and, very often, was the first to hear when one of them vanished from the face of the waters without trace. So far as I knew he had no ties with the sea and his longest voyage was his annual passage from Dover to Calais on his way to Basel where, for nearly a quarter of a century, he carried on an austere and, as it turned out, abortive courtship of a watchmaker's daughter. He kept her portrait on the wall of his little room among the maps and Admiralty charts giving a strange feminine fragrance to the place almost as startling, I used to think, as the sight of a dairymaid would be on the deck of a destroyer. But I must not let these fancies lure me on lest I finish up like Andrew Marvell stumbling on melons beyond the Mexique bay.

What really brought old Churchill back to my mind was a British United Press message from Atlanta in Georgia where Bobby Jones, Wallace Beery and Brer Fox came from. It was all about an amazing bed invented by a South Carolina colonel which would have pleased Churchill no end. The Carolina bed has high walls of acoustic wood to keep out noise and a partition in the centre which the sleepers can raise with a winch when they get bored with each other. On the female side of the bed there is an electric massage machine and a perfume spray battery, while the male side is equipped with electric razors and toothbrushes. Then there is a ceiling screen for films and television and a series of buttons which release selected scents which give the sleeping sybarites the illusion of being in Dixie or California. There are even the scents of smoked ham or fresh fish for those who want to feel they are in Maryland or Maine.

In a more elaborate way this reminded me of the bed in which I found my friend Churchill as he lay dying a very happy man. He had no fancy fragrances to remind him of Devon but by a cunning arrangement of ropes and pulleys he could pull in everything he wanted from all over the room without ever leaving his bed. And, what the Carolina colonel seems to have forgotten, Churchill's couch was flanked by two firkins, one of beer and the other of sherry, and at the back of his head he had a glass barrel of whisky and a cabinet of cigars. On Saturday morning when he had seen his last ship safely into port he would return to Clapham—go to bed and stay there till Monday night when he would be back in his watch-tower with the watchmaker's daughter presiding once more—with me as his powder monkey—over the landfalls and departures of the great and little ships. It's queer isn't it what funny memories can be stirred by a story from Carolina?

*January 20th,* 1951

## A MELODIOUS GHOST

IT must have been a surprise to many people—even to those who call themselves, so quaintly, the "profession"—to hear that the composer of "Nellie Dean" and "Sweet Adeline" has just died in New York.

For I have always thought of the composer of "Nellie Dean" and "Sweet Adeline" as a belated Victorian ballad-monger who somehow survived the raillery of Gilbert and Sullivan and the fin de siècle fantaisistes, and passed away in 1910 along with King Edward and Mark Twain to the roll of Alexander's ragtime drums. There is no record that he ever wrote anything like "Nellie Dean" or "Sweet Adeline" again.

It is odd to think of this melodious old man living on among the bright lights of Broadway writing away, no doubt for dear life, but never again recapturing the first fine careless rapture in which he made Nell and Adeline immortal with a song. "Nellie Dean" was the first music-hall song I ever heard, except on a phonograph, for in my young days there were no such things as theatres north of Aberdeen. It was in Sheffield that I first heard the song, in 1915. And apart altogether from the eager young loveliness of Gertie Gitana, who was like a wild rose in those days, I shall never forget that night. For it was also the first time I ever saw a grown-up civilian in kilts, except for an old Welsh hermit who used to play Beethoven on the bagpipes in an old ruin near Wick called Proudfoot Castle, overlooking what Robert Louis Stevenson, who hated the place bitterly, described as the meanest of men's towns on the baldest of God's bays. The psychiatrists—at least the Hollywood variety—say that every individual has a different response to a familiar tune. I don't know about that, but I do know that, except for perfumes, there is nothing like an old melody for bringing back the past. Just watch the look that comes into your grandmother's eyes when they play the "Merry Widow Waltz" or "Nights of Gladness" on the wireless! Even if music is no longer the food of love as it was in Illyria it is certainly the handmaiden of memory. There is no way of measuring the benefit people like Harry Armstrong bestow on mankind. If I were asked to name the man who has given most pleasure to the greatest number of people during my lifetime I should say it was Irving Berlin. I can hear my highbrow friends laughing at that, but it does not alarm me. For, as Keir Hardie used to say about the poor, God must love the lowbrows or he wouldn't have made so many of them. Until I read it the other day I didn't even know that Armstrong wrote "Sweet Adeline." I always supposed that it was one of the early Victorian ballads like "Genevieve" and "Just a Song at Twilight" which are sung today only by students on the spree, industrial correspondents, Lord Citrine and football fans on the way home in the charabanc. It is "Nellie Dean" that I shall always love. Most people, I fancy, when they listen to it think of love's young dream in a lilac sunbonnet—Gertie Gitana swinging it will remain for ever in my heart—and hear the music of the mill wheels and the harnessed waters. To me it has a deeper significance. It will always bring back that far-off winter night in Sheffield and the smell of fish and chips in the gallery and—as the psychiatrists say—by association, the memory of that stormy headland with the seagulls wheeling round the ruined keep and a wild-eyed Welshman hurling Beethoven back at Boreas in the teeth of the gale.

*March 2nd*, 1951

## OLD JONESY TURNS UP

WHEN I was in Flanders in the first World War serving as a Scot in an Irish division, I had a Welsh sergeant named Jones who was a great and, in his way, glorious character. He was an immense globular giant of a man, with a great purple circular face and sensational waxed mustachios, curled like two question marks on each side of his nose, which gave him an odd Mephistophelean air. His chest, which was radiant with ribbons, was like a hogshead, his legs like barrels and his enormous hands—with which he could make a tin whistle sound like the pipes of Pan—were like bunches of bloodshot bananas. Beneath his fierce Gargantuan façade, however, he had a heart of gold, the soul of a saint and the mind of a child.

When I first met him in Hesdin, where Petain was born, he was still basking in the grisly glory of having been the last man with the heroic Gen. Wauchope when he was killed at Magersfontein—or was it the Modder River?—in the South African War. Sgt. Jones always made a great thing of this episode, which was the big event of his life, and he retold the tragic tale nearly every night in the canteen, especially when there were any new recruits about. "Died in these very arms," he would say stretching his huge fists as if he were measuring an invisible fish, "breathed his last and expired, he did, and his last words to me were, 'Take care of yourself, Jones, don't let the so-and-so's get you.'" The Irish and Scots being romantics like himself, used to humour him, but the Cockneys were always making fun of him and urging him to tell them what the general really said. After a while the dying words of Wauchope became as fruitful a source of speculation with us as the *mot de Cambronne* at Waterloo still is with the historians. But Sergeant Jones was a Methodist—though he could sink his pint with the worst of us—and he had a prim spinsterish delicacy which prevented him from repeating his hero's dying words.

All that was over 30 years ago and I had almost forgotten him until the other day when I was clearing out an old chest filled with faded photographs, menus, hotel bills and all those foolish things my friend Jack Strachey sings so nostalgically about. Among this pile of sentimental rubbish I came across a bundle of old theatre programmes. And there for no reason at all, among the stars of long ago, was old Jonesy glowering at me in sepia like one of those Italian balloons with big round saucy eyes and curly moustaches painted on them. I remember the day he had that picture taken very well. It was in Amiens, just before the Battle of the Somme. We had a long week-end leave and the Sergeant, who, in spite of his chapel upbringing was not insensible to the tender passion, had what he called a "rendezvous with an inamorata." And he had this likeness taken to leave with her when the Higher Command sent him from her arms to some less amorous corner of a foreign field.

He took me one day to meet his loved one. She was a thin, nervous little widow with nothing in the world but a sewing machine, two pallid little daughters and Sergeant Jones. Had things turned out differently she would today have been living in the Rhondda a shy old lady with a sad smile, a queer accent and strange mysteries in her eyes. But it was not to be. When we got back to the line Sergeant Jones was killed. And when I got to Amiens three months later to give Madeleine a few sentimental souvenirs he had asked me to take to her, she was not there. The little cottage with the sewing machine in the window was just a hole in the ground and Madeleine and the two little girls had gone, like Hans Breitmann, into the *ewigkeit*. I cannot even remember which town Sergeant Jones came from, but I know that if there is a place in Paradise for fat men he will be there with Falstaff, Friar Tuck, Dr. Johnson and Chesterton. And if there is a canteen there he will be getting them into a corner and saying to them, "Died in these very arms, he did."

It's queer what you can find at the bottom of an old trunk!

*December 8th,* 1951

# MR. CARTWRIGHT'S SCOOP

ROUND about a quarter of a century ago when mah-jongg and hansom cabs were going out and crossword puzzles and double-decker buses were coming in, there was a strange, quiet, shabby man who used to hang about the Fleet Street taverns. His name was Cartwright. He appeared to have no home or relations, and he looked, in his shiny, snuff-stained suit and greasy bowler hat, like one of those minor characters in Dickens who dart about for a few pages, between the legs of the great gargoyles and grotesques like Micawber and Mr. Guppy, and then vanish for ever with a careless flourish of that prodigal pen.

Old Cartwright has been dead for some years now, but he became a ghost long before he died—as so many Fleet Street characters do—a sort of seedy left-over from the Grub Street days, with nothing left about them but a sour smell of beer and cigarette ends, in the shabby sunset of their former glory. There was a bleak wintry dignity in his bearing, in spite of his patched shoes and celluloid collar, and, though we all knew he had been somebody in his time, none of us had the courage or the cruelty to ask him about it. His favourite haunt was the sawdust bar of the Cheshire Cheese where he used to meet worthies like T. W. H. Crosland—an even grubbier ghost than himself—and Harold Lake, who wrote "I Hear You Calling Me" on the back of one of the famous steak and lark pie menus.

There it was, one autumn night, in the corner by the fire where old William the waiter used to shout for Mr. Labouchere's pudding and Mr. Sala's cigar, that Cartwright lifted the veil from his mysterious past. He raised just a little corner of it, it is true, but oh, as Sir Max would say, how revealing! It was the night that Queen Alexandra died, and the talk was all about newspaper scoops and "splash" stories. We were comparing such epics as de Blowitz's balloon dispatches from beleaguered Paris in 1870, Hugh Martin's "beat" on the death of Edward the Seventh, and Philip Gibbs' exposure of Dr. Cook, the Ananias of the Arctic, when Cartwright spoke. He suddenly piped up in a thin, reedy voice: "I had a scoop once, you know!" It was like a bombshell. The old ghost was gratified by the sensation he had caused, and continued: "Oh yes, it was quite a big thing at the time, very big indeed."

Then he proceeded to tell us how he was the first newspaper man to find out that Capt. O'Shea was to bring divorce proceedings against his wife and to name Mr. Parnell as co-respondent. He told us how he tracked the captain down to a poky little villa in Brighton which was filled with aspidistras, horsehair sofas, esparto grass in huge jars and pictures framed in sea shells and bits of broken looking-glass. Capt. O'Shea, instead of throwing Cartwright into the street, as he feared, cracked a bottle of port and gave him the whole story, which became the greatest political sensation of the decade. And when his notebook was full the captain summoned a growler and sent him to the station.

But this was not all! Like a good reporter of the old style, he kept the real surprise to the end. For this was in the days before the drama of the morning paper was destroyed by the dull device of putting everything in the opening paragraph. "You see," he said, as he picked up his tankard, "the reason I remember it so well is that on my way back to London I shared a compartment with George Meredith and a drunken woman who kept calling the poet 'an old geezer.' When we got to Victoria Mr. Meredith asked me to have dinner with him at his club, after which I defeated him at chess and then went back to Fleet Street with the Parnell story just in time for the first edition." Then he emptied his tankard and retired once more behind his veil. He never lifted it again except for one tiny peep when I asked him, some months later, to tell me more about his meeting with Capt. O'Shea. He looked at me in his wintry way for a long time and said, slowly: "There is nothing more to say except that it was very bad port." I may, I hope, be wrong, but I fear I shall not meet anybody like Cartwright in the Cheese tonight.

*December 15th,* 1951

# PART FIVE

# Mackay Abroad

## A DANDER ROUND THE TOWN

DUBLIN.

WHEN I flung wide my magic casement this morning and looked forth upon this lovely, thrilling city, the horse-cabs, with their spokes spinning like silver, were jingling down from Stephen's Green to Trinity. Far off on the way to the river a fiddler was playing "Caro Nome," from "Rigoletto," and a loudspeaker went blaring by, shouting, "Give the reins to Sean MacBride." As I had nothing on hand till I met Sean O'Faolain for lunch at the Bailey, I decided to follow Leopold Bloom and go for a dander round the town. Needless to say I avoided the extravagant eccentricities of Joyce's hatless wanderer and made more of a literary than an alcoholic odyssey of it. After all this is the city of Swift, Sheridan, Sterne, Wilde, Shaw, Synge, Yeats, Stephens, O'Casey and all the Moores, to say nothing of Balfe, Burke, creepy-crawly Le Fanu and the great Bishop Berkeley, who held the healthy, if then vainglorious, view that anything he could not think about did not exist.

I had looked first at Swift and his "Stella," lying side by side in St. Patrick's, and then went in search of Shaw. Believe it or not, his famous fantasy about the black girl in search of God has just been certified by the Irish censor as fit for human consumption, as if it were a leg of beef. I found his birthplace in Synge Street, but, so far as Dublin is concerned, it is just another house. There is nothing anywhere to show that one of the mightiest spirits of all time first sprang to life in this drab street. As I was pondering on this, six fat bullocks went by on their way to the shambles, and, as I watched them stumbling past, with their breath making woolly clouds of steam, it seemed to be Dublin's comment on her greatest living son.

This end of Dublin is a bewildering and shameless mess of squalor and splendour. Thousands of people huddled together in magnificent middens with beautiful doorways which would look lovely even in

Florence or Verona. In one of those doorways I overheard an old woman say to a seedy man with a rimless greasy bowler and celluloid collar: "Sure 'twill be better for you wid a jury. They'll clip the wing o' the ould judge." Outside the house where Tom Moore was born I saw an elegant funeral held up by a flock of sheep. One of the women mourners was feeding her infant as if she were anxious to ensure that the tragedy of man will go on for at least another generation.

It was in Aungier Street, too, that I came across a hideous little hunchback manikin with a head like a sea buoy. He goggled at me and turned into an enormous barn of a place where the Dublin poor are doing their 40 hours' devotions and paying their pennies to keep His Holiness on his throne. I followed him, and there he was on his knees with his hideous head bowed in reverence before the Blessed Virgin in her blue snood. His simple, helpless happiness touched something in my heathen heart, and I turned away and left him there in rapt communion with the only grace and loveliness he will ever find on this earth. Maybe, for all I know, he was seeing golden visions that are denied to the likes of me.

*January 30th*, 1948

# SHAKING HANDS WITH A CRUSADER

DUBLIN.

IT was an Ulsterman, Cathal O'Shannon, Lilliputian leader of the Irish trade unions, who sent me to shake hands with the Cœur de Lion's Crusader in the dim, cold, spider-haunted vaults of St. Michan's, the oldest and eeriest of Ireland's churches. Except for that creepy catacomb in Bordeaux, where the skeletons of guillotined Girondists stand in flood-lit niches with their heads tucked underneath their arms I have never seen such a macabre place. They did not need to tell me Sheridan Le Fanu worshipped here. There is some strange quality in the air of St. Michan's which mummifies the dead and has preserved some of them for nearly 1,000 years. So there I was handling skulls just like Hamlet, and stroking shin bones of lords and ladies gay who fought, dreamed, wenched and wassailed on Liffey's banks before even Strongbow came to make the place safer for de Valera. The Crusader is wonderfully well preserved, and according to custom I shook him by the hand.

Five minutes later I passed the house where Napper Tandy was born and the queer fancy struck me—maybe he, too, had greeted the Crusader and thus by a grisly, apostolic succession I could claim that the immortal rebel "took me by the hand." And I wondered at the odd fate which led Napper from his dusty vault to roam the world and die at last in far-away Bordeaux and be buried in that other strange sepulchre among the headless men of the Gironde. Inevitably one of the wags inquired if the Crusader had been to vote, and the sexton said the usual arrangements had been made. Then we saw the spinet which Handel played in this church when he came here in 1742 for the world première of the "Messiah," which was first produced in Fishamble Street with the divine composer on the rostrum. When I passed the place last night three tipsy colleens were rolling by singing "Mammy."

Perhaps the queerest thing about St. Michan's is the mystery of the spiders' webs. These webs are as thick and heavy as velvet blankets and the problem is where did the spiders get the food to make them strong enough to spin the webs? They are the only living things in the vaults and they never touch the corpses. There is only one explanation—and this is where Le Fanu comes in again—they live by eating each other just like human beings, as one of the visitors said to the sexton. It was a relief to get out once more into the crisp Dublin air and rejoin O'Shannon in one of the famous literary taverns of the town where poets, playwrights and painters are as thick as spivs in Charing Cross Road.

There never was such a town for talk and most of it seems to spin round O'Shannon who is a bright bird-like little fellow exactly like Lord Beveridge looked at through the wrong end of a telescope. I found him with two of Ireland's greatest poets discussing why Jim Larkin could not make Socialism go in Ireland. The election results were coming in by this time, but nobody cared two hoots. When I told them where I had been somebody said, "Do you know that Bernard Shaw is buried in another vault in Merrion Square and that they are going to resurrect him when he dies?" But I will have to tell you about that when, Almighty and Aer Lingus willing, I get back to London on Monday.

*February 6th,* 1948

## THEY SELL AIR AS A SIDE LINE

CHICAGO.

IT was a wall-eyed Welsh barman in Wabash Avenue who told me the most profitable business nowadays in Chicago is the sale of air. Not hot air or liquid air, or even the air on the G string for which the Chicago burlesques are famous, but just plain, ordinary air that folks breathe. It made me happy to hear this, for in my youth I once suggested to my Socialist friends that the best way to deal with the Tory landowners was for the Socialists to stake claims in the air and charge people for breathing it, just as the squires charged the workers for living on their land. And it surprises me to hear that it was not Al Capone, who had a genius for milking mankind, who first thought of selling air, but a decent respectable freight-carrying company which sells it as a side line.

This company, which carries most of Chicago's heavy truck traffic in underground tunnels, had to pump millions of cubic feet of air into the workings every day to keep the wage slaves alive. After a while they discovered they had far too much air on their hands. So one bright boy on the board proposed they should sell it by the cubic foot to theatres, night clubs, hotels, shops and basement offices. And such is the power of simple ideas that nearly everybody now buys their air from the Tunnel Company in spite of the fact that Chicago is so full of free air that they call it "The Windy City." In fact, the company is making so much money out of thin air that they are seriously considering packing up the freight business altogether. I believe these boys could sell air at the top of Ben Nevis.

It was the Welsh gin slinger, too, who told me about the church in the sky round the corner from his boisterous boozer. It is called the Chicago Temple and it is quite literally built in the sky, perched on top of a skyscraper, steeple and all, nearly a furlong above the busiest street corner in the world. A Methodist chapel to begin with, it was opened in 1834 by a few wandering Welshmen and has been open ever since. At first it was just a shack on the lake shore, but the years rolled by and the lake rolled back and the huge fierce brawling city grew up with all its wealth and wickedness around the quiet little chapel. Time and again the hog-butchers and money-changers tried to get the disturbing place moved from their avaricious path. This was not easy, however, for the wily Welsh worshippers a century ago got a perpetual title deed granting them the site "for religious purposes for ever."

Now in Chicago "ever" is a very short time. Even the eternal verities have a job of it to keep going. But the Methodists were too tough for the tycoons and in the end big business had to compromise. Capitalism made a truce with religion and it was agreed that whatever happened that little bethel would stay on that spot. That is why it is now way up in the sky nearly as near Heaven as Colonel McCormick. For it is part of the bargain between the Methodists and the money-changers that however high that skyscraper goes, the church goes up with it. And so, as the years go by, this curious church will rise closer and closer to Heaven pushed there by the ever-expanding hordes of Jewish, Catholic, Episcopalian and even Confucian money-spinners who weave their webs on the first forty floors.

*July 5th*, 1948

## LITTLE LOVELINESS

### HOLLYWOOD.

SHE joined the train at North Platte, where Buffalo Bill used to live when he wasn't on the trail to Tientsin or Budleigh Salterton and she left it at Sacramento where the gold rush began a hundred years ago. That means we had to put up with her boisterous charm for the best part of two days. She was a baby starlet from Hollywood who had been on location on Buffalo Bill's ranch and she was indeed a "dish" as they say in San Francisco. A beautiful bore, shimmering in mother-of-pearl silk which clung to her lethal loveliness like a swim-suit, she wriggled around the club car and the diner like an odious glittering snake radiating regulation switched-on studio smiles and exuding erotic perfume and synthetic sex-appeal like a cuttle-fish. She was what Aeschylus—believe it or not—in the Agamemnon calls "a dumb fair piece," exquisite, creamy and curvaceous. And she laughed and giggled and made her eyes dance all the time. She laughed all the way through Wyoming and Nevada. What she was doing as we went through Utah I cannot say, for I was sound asleep.

The first thing I heard when I woke up at Elko, in Nevada, was the silvery ripple of her girlish laughter. She was projecting her fatal charms at a group of cowboys who looked as if they had been making

a night of it in warmer company than hers in that incredible fun-fair in the desert. Some hours later, when we got up into the high sierras, she clapped her little pink gold-tipped hands and gurgled: "Goo, darling"—that was me—"look, it's real snow." I said I was glad to hear it, as I thought at first it was one of D. W. Griffith's old salt and cotton wool sets left over from "The Birth of a Nation." But she insisted it was real snow. Once I escaped from her and joined the lady who was reading about molluscs. 'Twas all in vain. Little Loveliness had heard by this time I was an English newspaper man and she wanted me to tell her what chance she would have of making a hit in London. I told her she would be a "wow," but I didn't say in which part of London her peculiar talents would be recognised.

She was pleased with this and when I said I came from Edinburgh she asked if that was in London too. I said, no, it was in Glasgow. She brightened up at this and said she knew a song about Glasgow. Then I tried reading "Tristram Shandy," but she wanted to know what it was about. I told her it was about everything and nothing, that it was written by a parson and was full of naughty jokes. I even told her one of them, but she just looked lovely and dumb and asked me to explain it to her. At this the mollusc woman tried to save the day by asking if I had seen Olivier's "Hamlet." This was no good. Peaches-and-cream wanted to know what this was about too.

At Reno, where we stretched our legs for ten minutes, she showed me the hotel where she stayed "the first time" she was divorced. She will use Las Vegas next time, as she says the casino is more comfortable there and it's nearer Hollywood. The dear thing should settle in Reno or Las Vegas. It will save so much travelling. The last I saw of her she was standing on Sacramento platform with her coloured maid beside a mountain of trunks and suitcases looking lovelier, deadlier and dumber than ever.

*July 9th,* 1948

# DRY WELCOME FROM LAND OF SHACKSPEARE

## GOLDEN ARROW.

MADAME and Monsieur Dupont belong to the ancient city of Bergerac, in the Dordogne, where the truffles and the nuts and the wine come from. They have just been married and are having their honeymoon in what they described to me with great excitement as "Shackspeare's Country." I knew they came from Bergerac because I saw it on their luggage.

I saw them first struggling with their cases along the platform at the Gare du Nord and I helped Madame on to the Golden Arrow with as much Highland gallantry as I could summon up with a raincoat over one arm and a Port Salut cheese under the other. It was then I saw they came from Cyrano's home town, but I did not speak to them until I met them in mid-Channel six hours later leaning against the wind on the boat deck of the British Railways flagship S.S. Invicta. They were chattering away happily in Dordogne English and watching a jolly school of glistening porpoises gambolling in the flashing, sun-shot wash of a big Dutchman who had just crossed our bows and was vanishing into the sunset on his way to Sourabaya and the palmgreen shores. Madame was a perfect picture of windswept loveliness, but she didn't know the English word for *marsouin*. Plucking up my courage I advanced boldly and said: "Porpoise, madame"!

If they really came from Bergerac, I said to myself, they will understand. After all, I thought, a Mackay has as much panache in his way as a Cyrano and if that immortal swashbuckler could poke his famous nose into everybody's business why can't I do the same with my broken if less illustrious one? It came off. Soon we were chatting away and waving our arms in the finest Dordogne fashion about Bergerac and Wick and Cyrano and Burns, and by the time "Shackspeare's" Cliff came glimmering over the horizon we were going at it as if we had known each other all our lives.

Hitherto, all I knew about Bergerac apart from Cyrano was that my old friend Emile Haon, who runs an auberge in Fleet Street, was born there, and that Margaret of Navarre—who invented the short story—once washed her feet in the river there after trampling grapes in the market square. To me it was always a story book city that existed only in the songs of the troubadours. But Madame and Monsieur Dupont assure me it is a very real place indeed and informed me, quite seriously, that I had committed a very grave crime by passing it by to spend my holiday in such meretricious dumps as Nice and Monte Carlo. I promised it would not happen again and they forgave me "for the sake of Shackspeare" provided I stood them a glass of English beer when the boat got to Dover.

Now, Mr. Barnes, I want you to listen, Sir Eustace Missenden will you pay attention, and my Lord Inman, will you lend an ear? I want to tell you how "Shackspeare's country" welcomed those two nice people from Bergerac on their first visit to a land they love. We got through the Customs, parked our bags and made for the bar. It was 5.45 p.m. The shelves were gay with all the famous beers, and, feeling proud of Old Mother England, I ordered three of the best. "Sorry," said Hebe behind the bar. "We don't open till 6.30." "When does the train leave?" "At 6.30," she replied. I knew then I was back home. As the train pulled out Hebe opened up but then there were no customers. "Shackspeare," thou shouldst be living at this hour! I wonder what Cyrano would have done about it!

*October 12th, 1948*

# THE CHAIR IN ROOM 108

## DUESSELDORF.

ACCORDING to the programme I mapped out when I left Holland this column today should have been headed "Frankfurt, Monday." For it was my intention to spend the week-end in Goethe's home town, where they are preparing to celebrate the bicentenary of the birth of that remarkable man. I was eager also to see how the Americans were running their corner of the Control Commission for Germany—the C.C.G.—which the German comedians refer to as the "Coca Cola Government." But it was not to be. My car broke down on what appeared to me to be the loneliest stretch of road between Inverness and Ispahan.

Fortunately my fellow-traveller and *News Chronicle* colleague, Norman Clark, had been that way before when he came through with Patton, so we were soon in the village of Neustadt Wien in front of a plate of liverwurst and cucumber which seems to be the thing to eat in this part of the world. Next door to the café, they told us, lived the village doctor, whose wife comes from Stoke Newington, but unfortunately they were not at home.

Neustadt is an extraordinary little town. Unless my ageing eyes deceived me, it seemed to be almost entirely inhabited by Jane Russells and little bandy-legged men with big noses like Schnozzle Durante. It was the eve of Ascension Day, and when we strolled into the churchyard the chestnut trees were filled with girls in pretty frocks and white calf-length stockings with silver tasselled bells on them. They were plucking branches of red chestnut candles to strew on the streets for next day's procession of maidens. Ascension Day in the Rhineland is not only a religious festival. For the women and girls it is the first day of the year when they can show off their summer frocks, and for the men it is a kind of sacred saturnalia. It is the one day in the year—like Fathers' Day in America—when the men can do no wrong. They can get as drunk as they like, and if their wives catch them kissing frauleins under the linden trees they just laugh and cry the German equivalent of "Oh! la! la!" Even if he comes home late with a bellyful of Liebfraumilch nobody cares, for it is his day, and he is welcomed with encouraging smiles and plates of sauerkraut as if he were the prodigal son himself.

Chesterton, who was not very fond of the Germans, would have liked this place. It is a nice, quiet homely little town—gemuchlicht is the German word for it, I believe—where everybody knows everybody else, where the windows are full of eggs, dachshunds ripple about the streets like animated fur boas, sloe-eyed gypsy girls sell cherries in coloured bags, and the priest and the protestant parson share a bottle of the good Rhine wine together as the sun goes down over Luxemburg and the patient bullocks come home from the fields with their over-laden wains clattering on the cobbles behind them.

The garage people after taking the car to pieces and throwing the bits all over the village, announced that it would take eight hours and ten times as many marks to put it together again. So there was nothing for it but to send for another car, which took two hours to reach us. As a result of this masterpiece of Mackay organisation we were back in Duesseldorf nine hours after we had left it, as I thought for the last time. But before we turned back we went on for a few miles to St. Goar to see the famous Lorelei Rock, which Heine wrote his lovely poem about, and the lady at the inn where Wagner used to sit pointed out to us the pole in the river where the Rheingold is supposed to lie.

It is a lovely spot, but not nearly so impressive as Symonds Yat, on the Wye, which would have been coining dollars for Cripps if only Housman and Elgar had done for it what Heine and Wagner did for the Lorelei. As I have frequently observed in this column, there is an Emersonian element in the affairs of man by which every calamity is accompanied by a corresponding compensation. On this occasion it was the story of Room 108. If that mediaeval Mercedes had not broken down I would not have heard how the war really began in that unpretentious little sitting-room on the second floor of the Park Hotel. This famous hotel is now called York House, and it is a kind of home from home for the British colony in Duesseldorf where Very Important and Exceedingly Bored Persons live on British rations and sit around in huge green armchairs supping gin or thin tea or reading yesterday's *Times* or last week's *Tatler*.

We got back just in time for dinner, and afterwards as we had coffee in Room 108 Peter, the barman, said to me, "You are sitting in Hitler's chair." "How can that be?" I asked. "Hitler was never in Duesseldorf." "Oh, yes he was," Peter replied, "and I served him. He had an orangeade and a chocolate eclair." Then he explained this was the famous secret conference between Hitler and the Ruhr magnates led by Herr Thyssen in 1932 just before the Nazis came to power. It was in this very room Thyssen promised to back Hitler with men, money and material if he suppressed the Socialists. After the meeting Hitler had to be smuggled out of the hotel by the tradesmen's entrance as there was a crowd in the Koenigsallee. Even so, somebody had a pot-shot at him which unfortunately missed.

It is a simple little room with two bad pictures, a hideous tapestry, and in spite of what Gracie Fields may say to the contrary, the largest aspidistra in the world. Peter also told me how Hitler had a row with Dr. Ley about drink and ordered him to stop supping whisky. Ley went to his doctor and got from him permission to have an occasional whisky in his tea. He came back to the Park Hotel all smiles and asked Peter to bring him a cup of tea and a bottle of Scotch.

*June 1st*, 1949

## TRIBUTE TO A SCOUNDREL

COPENHAGEN.

LIKE Hamlet himself, after his escape from the pirates, I am taking a long time to get to Elsinore. And when I do get there in the end let us pray that the wind may be in the south and not nor'-nor'-west. For on this journey of mine through the three kingdoms of Scandinavia it is just as well that I should know a hawk from a hand-saw. And if any Shakespearian pedant writes in to say that last word should be "Hernshaw" I will hand him over to my distinguished countrymen, Ivor Brown and Alan Dent, and so, again like Hamlet, sweep to my revenge. It was in the old state prison in Copenhagen that the indomitable Liverpool adventurer, James Norcross, was kept in chains for 32 years. Hamlet, I feel, will forgive us keeping him waiting a little longer so that we may halt a moment on the castle walls to pay a tribute to this gallant old scoundrel. Norcross, whose wild adventures on land and sea, in battle and the boudoir would make a rattling film, was the laughing cavalier of the sea—if you can fancy such a curious horse marine—and was ever ready for a fight with the men or a frolic with the ladies wherever his restless feet led him. He was born in Toxteth in 1688—the year William of Orange landed in Brixham—and after a wild romp round England he sailed away to Sweden and joined the Army there to fight the Danes. The Swedes were carrying on the war on orthodox lines with long sieges and short battles, but Norcross, who was not a Liverpool "Scowser" for nothing, had other ideas. Errol Flynn, the conqueror of Burma, had nothing on him. First he tried to capture the Danish Crown Prince but was captured and sentenced to death. While waiting to be shot he got away and swam for it. They caught him again at Malmo, but he escaped once more and got back to Sweden. By this time his Liverpool blood was up. He did not come from Mrs. Braddock's home town for nothing. "To hell with the Crown Prince," he said. "Let's have a crack at the king." He got back to Copenhagen with the aid of a coquette and was about to shoot the king when they grabbed him. This time the king was merciful and businesslike. Instead of beheading him he ordered the royal tormentors to give him a few turns of the thumbscrews, a wrench or two of the rack, a modicum of boiling oil and a few languid applications of red-hot irons. Apart from that they were told to be kind to him, and after a week or two of such

125

pleasantries Norcross was chained up in a wooden cage and slung out over the ramparts for the crowds to laugh at. The cage was just big enough for him to stand up in, but he took it all quite cheerfully and amused the crowds so much with some white mice which he tamed that they became very fond of him and used to give him tit-bits on holidays, very much as children throw buns to the bears in the Zoo. After 16 years of this a new king took him out of his cage, not so much because it gave pain to Norcross but because it gave pleasure to the people. But he did not do the big thing and set him free to go home to Liverpool. Oh, no! He merely took him inside the citadel and clapped him in a dark dungeon, where he languished for another 16 years before he died in the dark, alone and forgotten, in 1758. But, as you see, he was not altogether forgotten and here, nearly two centuries later, he has a column in the *News Chronicle* all to himself. And perhaps tonight in the Liverpool Press Club, where there are still a few intrepid adventurers left, my friends Jack Yeadon and Don Christie may raise a shadowy glass to old Jim Norcross, who, had he only lived in their time, would have been meat and drink to them. The moral of this story, if it has a moral at all, is that it doesn't pay to poke your nose into other people's wars and that if you have a good job on the Mersey the thing to do is to stick to it.

*May 9th,* 1950

## WHEN NORA BANGED THE DOOR . . . .

NORWAY.

IT was still bitterly cold when I said good-bye to Oslo and set out over Peer Gynt's mountains for Stockholm, the lovely city of Queen Christina and Gustavus Adolphus, where Greta Garbo and Ingrid Bergman were born, Descartes died, Strindberg went mad, Nobel invented dynamite, Jenny Lind first began to sing, Morgenröter invented the typewriter—blast him—and Ole Tandberg gave Baksi a pasting just after he had broken Bruce Woodcock's jaw.

The snow had nearly all gone, however, save for a few silvery wisps up among the pines, and a funeral fringe of sooty slush around the airfield. This made things more unpleasant for as that sapient troubadour Ogden Nash once put it, snow, like inebriation, is very pleasing when it is coming, but very unpleasing when it is going. Though I was glad to be going and excited to think that in two hours I would be in the Venice of the North for the first time, I was reluctant to leave Oslo without having *tasted* more of it. It could not possibly, I thought, be as dull as I found it all the time, and surely there were more places than Blom's fascinating eating house where people met and drank and looked merry. After all, it was Ibsen's town and the great gales of that angry iconoclast are still blowing through the world. It was here in this small town among the woods and waters remote from the surge and clamour of the glittering world of wealth and fashion that the sour-faced druggist's apprentice suddenly broke away from his carboys and ointment pots and revolutionised the theatre.

It was hard to believe as I walked through this very ordinary town —it is a kind of a cross between Lowestoft and Leamington Spa— that Hedda Gabler and Nora Helmer lived here and that it was pro- bably in that drab street that Nora walked out of the Doll's House slamming the door behind her with a bang that still—as G. B. S. says —reverberates throughout Europe. That bang started something. It was the clarion call to women everywhere. It set the Pankhursts and the Pethick Lawrences marching to Trafalgar Square, it sent Madame Curie from the laundry to the laboratory, made Emily Davison fling herself in front of the horses at Epsom, put Madame Chiang at the head of a nation, sent Amy Johnson into the sky and Edith Cavell into her grave and placed Mrs. Braddock and Barbara Castle on the green benches at Westminster.

Every typist who paints her lips and goes to Brighton on the back of her boy friend's bike, every Fleet Street siren who quaffs her pint at the Women's Press Club, every bachelor girl who "leads her own life" as the saying is, and every woman everywhere who claims equality and the rate for the job, does so because of that old man in Oslo with the mutton-chop whiskers and the elastic-sided boots. I am sorry to keep harping on those boots but to my mind they are essential to the understanding of Ibsen just as Jaeger jackets and carrot and cauli- flower cutlets are essential to the understanding of Shaw. Those elastic-sided boots meant that the saddles and spurs, cloak and dagger days were over and that the reign of realism had begun.

Well, all that started in this little town—or rather in a still smaller town nearby called Skien—exactly one hundred years ago. The story has never been told till now how Ibsen started. He was an apothecary's apprentice and in 1848 under the emotional urge of the Paris revolution he wrote a play which he called "Catiline." It was about the struggle between Cicero and Catiline, and young Ibsen—his head full of revolutionary fire—took the side of the conspirators. He signed the play "Brynjolf Bjarne" and as nobody would have anything to do with it he published it himself. He printed 250 copies but sold only 45. So he sold the remaining 205 copies to a ship's chandler, who wrapped soap and candles in them.

To get a first edition of "Catiline" now you have to pay at least £50. From all accounts it is a bad play full of revolutionary ranting and rhetoric. It was still a long way from the Boyg and the Button Moulder Brand and the Master Builder, but it was also a long way from the old blood-thirsty Nordic sagas which up till then was all Norway had in the way of drama except for Holberg, who was really a Dane. We should be thankful to Ibsen for putting a stop to that kind of thing. In any event, he had to make a start sometime and writing "Catiline" was better than mixing poultices for big blonde hypochondriacs in Bergen. And he had to earn something to pay for those boots!

*June 3rd,* 1950

## THE FIREFLY FISHERS OF CAMOGLI
### SORI.

TEMPTING as that radiant queen of cities is, we did not linger long in La Superba. For, lovely though she looked in the evening glow, glittering in crimson and gold on the blue breast of the sea, Genoa was not our goal. We were bound for Sori and a house called The Swallows, or Le Rondini, as the ignorant Italians say. And so, as the sun slid down over Spain to warm the convent windows in faraway Castile, we said good-bye to Columbus and took the road to Rome.

Sori—or what the Kesselring kids have left of it—is an odd squirming little town with two churches, a pleasant little plage, a bookshop entirely devoted to the works of Peter Cheyney, a post office which is also the G.H.Q. of the Communist Party, and a dried-up river bed. The Swallows turned out to be a lovely cool old house hanging on a

hill among the oranges high up above the gulf as it sweeps round to
Rapallo and Santa Margherita. When we arrived the night was
dancing deliriously with weird winking lights for all the world like
the ju ju flickerings which haunt the Emperor Jones in Eugene
O'Neill's play. These were the firefly fishers of Camogli, who attract
the sardines by fixing fierce lamps on the prows of their boats. This
quaint unspoiled fishing port is the birthplace of Schiaffino, who
carried the flag for Garibaldi and "The Thousand" and it never went
Fascist.

Looking through the guest book in the 'nineties I found that
Henry James was a Rondini regular and used to meet Alice Meynell,
the poetess, there, and my favourite woman writer, "Vernon Lee,"
who signed the book in her real name, Violet Paget. Then there were
Margaret Brooke, Ranee of Sarawak; the Count Karolyi; Hadow the
music man; Professor Saleeby, and, in 1893, Capt. John Jellicoe, R.N.
One day with Sean O'Faolain, the Irish writer, we went to see the
tombs of the Dorias in the old monastery in the rock at San Fruttuoso.
These merchant rajahs of the Renaissance were bigger buccaneers
than Drake. We never reached Viareggio, for the bus broke down in
Rapallo. But the thing that lingers most in my mind is the patient little
salamander—really a gecko—who lives upside down on the ceiling of
the Rondini veranda. He lives on moths, who live on flies, who live on
midges. Which—as the old ballad of "Ilkla Moor Baht 'At" reminds
us—is very human indeed of the gecko.

*September 13th,* 1947

# PHOTO-FINNISH

## HELSINKI.

TAKE my advice and have a long deep breath before you start
on this column today. For it promises to turn out a wild helter-
skelter inconsequential affair such as Mr. Jingle might dictate to
Mrs. Nickleby beside the waters that come down at Lodore. This is
not my fault as the Editor asks me to squeeze everything I found out
about Finland into one compact, comprehensive article. There has

been nothing like this since Procrustes—who would have made an admirable make-up man on a paper—used to chop pieces off his guests to make them fit the bed, or at any rate, since "The Night at the Opera" when the Marx Brothers crammed everything in the Queen Mary, from the captain to the ship's cat, into one small three-by-four cabin. Orders is orders, however, so hold everything! Here goes!! Before I was half an hour in Finland I had found out the following things about the place and its people.

The Finns have been at war with Russia 73 times. There are 3,737,800 Finns and 97 per cent of them are Lutherans. There are more Mohammedans than Roman Catholics and two out of every hundred people are orthodox in the Greek manner. Ten per cent of the people speak Swedish. If the Russians invade Finland again the Finns will fight to the last man. But they want to be friends. The Finns are the best-read people in Europe and the finest bookshop in the world is in Helsinki. I tried them on everything I could think of and they had it. They even had a guide to Skegness. Then they broke down. They didn't have one to Helsinki! There are twenty times as many dramatic societies in Finland as there are in England and their favourite British dramatists are Shakespeare, Shaw and Sheridan, with Priestley on their heels. Helsinki is not as big as Leeds, yet in the few days I was there I could have seen plays by Racine, Henry James, Ibsen, Euripides, Tennessee Williams, Lindgren, Arthur Miller, a piece by Shakespeare called "Kuinka Akapussi Kesytetaan"—which I think must be "The Taming of the Shrew"—Jose Greco and his Spanish dancers, and a thing called "Annie Get Your Gun" which was even funnier in Finnish than it was when I saw it in Paris at Easter as "Annie du Far West."

The world's greatest living composer, Sibelius, sculptor Waino Aaltonen and architect Aarvo Aalto are Finns, and the man who wrote the world's best seller last year, Mika Waltari—the book was "The Egyptian"—lives in Helsinki. Most of the world's fastest men and its slowest women live in Finland. The last of the old wind-jammers— there are only five of them left in the world—fly the Finnish flag, and the Stadium in Helsinki where the Olympic Games will be held in 1952 has the tallest tower in Europe, except that thing in Paris. There is a real *iron* Iron Curtain on the Russo-Finnish frontier at Porkkala, where my colleague Willie Forrest once stood in his famous white sheet and wrote the finest battle dispatch since the days of Archibald

Forbes. And in the canal corridor which the Soviet controls the trains run with closed blinds day and night. Nobody knows why.

Three-quarters of Finland is covered with trees, and in the remaining quarter there are more than a thousand lakes. There are dozens of kinds of hard drinks in Finland and most of them are made by mixing the trees with the water. The prices vary with the quality of the tree, birch being de luxe. One drink known as yellow-vin is guaranteed to make a rabbit sit up and spit in a bulldog's face. The Finns drink it as the French drink coca-cola. In all the main streets there are kiosks where you can buy beer and chocolates, but there are no proper pubs. Architecturally, Finland is the most original and exciting country in the world. The chief drawback about Finland is the language, which has no prepositions or personal pronouns. Ordering food is a bit of a trial. Supper is called Illallinen and if you want a steak or a sandwich you ask for a Häräseläke or an Alkupaloja. But, oh boys, oh boys, what a joy they are when they come. My favourite dish was Luumuhil-loketta Kuohukerman Kera, short for fruit salad and cream. Another trouble in Finland is the 1,000 mark note. It is so big that if you open it out in a high wind near the harbour you may be blown out to sea. And, of course, there are not enough of them. Finally, there are twenty-one Zilliacuses in the Helsinki phone book but no Smith. And there is no coca-cola anywhere. Not even on the cathedral roof. Which proves that the place is not as civilised as Milan, Perugia or Seville.

*June 24th*, 1950

## MYSTERY OF A HOLE

### BELGRADE.

THIS is the story of a hole in the ground. Not the kind of hole in the ground that Rupert Brooke listed, along with wet roofs and new-peeled sticks, among the things he had loved, but a meaningless man-made official hole with neither rhyme nor reason in it and devoid of beauty, mystery, purpose and romance.

Until a few days ago it was not there. Then it was there for an hour or two. Now, like the man upon the stair in the drunkard's ditty, it is not there again. In fact, it was, as Mr. Polly would have said, a "silly wheeze of a hole" which suddenly appeared like the Cheshire cat and then disappeared again. But it lasted long enough to create a minor international crisis in the Balkans. This then is the story of this hole as I heard it in Belgrade the other day. I cannot vouch for every detail, but as one who dug many similar holes in the Kaiser's war I accept the general pattern of the tale.

The hole was made in a field near Zagreb by the British section of the international brigade of young men and women who are helping Tito to finish his Five-Year Plan on time. One morning the British boys were told to dig a hole and they went at it with such zest that by sunset they had made the biggest artificial hole since Cheops dug up the stones for the pyramids. The Yugo-Slav commandant was so impressed that he gave the British a special flag and called them his shock troops. Next morning he sent them off to the woods to fell a record number of trees to celebrate their triumph. They marched off singing "Tipperary" with their axes on their shoulders determined to shave the landscape bare of every tree. But by the end of the day every tree in Croatia was still standing and the British were on strike.

What happened was this. On their way to the woods they had to pass the hole they made the day before. But when they got there the hole had disappeared. Back to camp they went and burst in on the Commandant. "What," they demanded, "have you done with our hole?" The Commandant didn't know, but promised to find out. It turned out that as soon as the British had finished the hole the Mexicans had marched out and filled it in again. This was too much for the boys of the bulldog breed. They had not come all the way from the Clyde and the Rhondda and given up their holidays to have their work undone by a gang of gauchos from Popocatepetl. So they downed axes, folded their arms and, in defiance of Deakin and the Devil, went on strike. They would not do another stroke until they got satisfaction. The Commandant was suave, but could do nothing himself. For Yugo-Slavia has passed a new law giving the workers control over such matters. The whole affair had to go before the works management committee. But this committee—like all committees the world over—washed their hands of it and appointed a special sub-committee to find out what had happened to the British hole.

The sub-committee acquitted everybody. The British were right to dig the hole ; the Mexicans were right to fill it in, the Commandant was right to refer it to the works management committee, that committee was right to have set up the sub-committee and generally speaking, the whole position was as right and satisfactory as it could be. They also pointed out that as there never had been any point in digging the hole, there was no harm in filling it in again. But the real pith of this Solomonic judgment came at the close. "Finally," the sub-committee declared, "we hold that in view of all the circumstances the decision of the British workers to go on strike was justified and dialectically correct." When I left Belgrade it had not been decided whether the hole should be dug once more or left as it was: a smooth magpie-haunted corner of a foreign field that is for ever—dialectically at least—England.

My suggestion is that the whole thing should be done all over again and fitted into the Five-Year Plan. Only this time the Mexicans should dig the hole and the British fill it in. And to think there are people who don't believe in Tom Sawyer; and Huckleberry Finn!

*September 30th*, 1950


## YOU CAN'T SLEEP FOR THE MICE

ROME.

THERE has probably been more nonsense written about Rome— especially by Englishmen—than about any other town on earth except, perhaps, Dublin, which is the real City of Beautiful Nonsense. Most people who have never been there think of Rome as a quiet city full of holy shrines and placid convents dreaming her eternal dream beside the Father of Waters ; a kind of overgrown Oxford with priests and seminaries instead of proctors and boathouses, and much older towers from which to whisper her enchantments. When they think of Rome physically they have a Byronic vision of mouldering monuments, crumbling columns and broken arches with rows of alabaster patricians in marble nightgowns glimmering in the ivory moonlight among the umbrella pines.

It is a beautiful dream and, thank goodness, there is plenty of reality behind it still. But there is another Rome that you hear very little about, the real living strident modern Rome that goes on among

the ancient ruins, the Rome of neon lights and nylons, English tea-shops and coca-cola parlours, the Rome of Togliatti and "topolinos," of Ingrid Bergman and Rossellini, beautiful bookshops, hideous slums and perfumed hotels, of the glittering Opera and the cheery music-hall where the star turn is called "The Bluebell Girls," as cute a battery of Bradford blondes as you will see south of the Brixton Empress.

For the truth is that Rome, for all its ancient grandeur and apostolic dignity, is one of the noisiest and most wearing cities in the world, exceeded only in my experience, by Chicago and Marseilles. And as for its monuments, though there are plenty of classical ones from Romulus and Remus down to Garibaldi and the monstrous abomination in honour of Victor Emmanuel, Rome is the only city which has a statue to a poet wearing a top hat.

It stands among the tramlines in front of Dante's house in Trastevere in the square called Sidney Sonnino and it commemorates Ghiaccino Belli, who was a kind of a cross between Burns and A. P. Herbert. He wrote racy poems about the common people and scandalised the priests. A few yards away in a lovely and rather dilapidated square, where I found the youngsters playing football with the great door of the oldest church in the world, Santa Maria in Trastevere, for a goal, I had a meal in Belli's favourite café where they make a macaroni called Angel's Hair which comes straight from Paradise. The waiter told me that his last foreign customer was Rita Hayworth, who went there last week—all on her own—for a plate of fettucini—that means ribbons—before going back to Hollywood. It is this constant jumble of ancient and modern that makes Rome such a startling and exciting city. You have only to turn a yard or two out of the main streets to see the neon lights reflected on the baths of Caracalla and the sky-signs winking on the Temple of the Vestal Virgins.

But at night it is the noise of Rome that surprises you most. It is mainly due to the fact that there is an anti-noise regulation in force. It is something on the lines of the order Hore-Belisha issued forbidding the blowing of motor horns at night. The Romans have gone one better than Belisha. You can't blow your horn there at all. This seems a queer rule in the city where Mussolini once lorded it and the sacred geese used to cackle in the Capitol. Being a law-abiding lot the Romans obey the rule. They never blow their horns. But they make ten times as much noise with their throttles and exhausts. The street

I lived in—called with grim irony "The Street of the Lion's Mouth" —appears to be the Roman Brooklands, and every night the local Nuvolaris went roaring up and down with their sloe-eyed inamoratas cheering them on. It was like trying to sleep in the Piazza in Covent Garden when the carrots and cucumbers are coming in. No wonder Verdi was so heavy on the brass at times. It was the only way to make himself heard.

*April 3rd,* 1951

# AND MOSES TOOK ME IN

CAIRO.

WHEN I am old and grey and full of sleep, to steal a phrase from W. B. Yeats who stole it from Ronsard, I shall still remember Moses. Long after I have forgotten all about Amenhotep the Third, King Farouk, and the sacred snakes of Saqqara I will be thinking about that dusky necromancer who found me wandering and took me in. Needless to say I am not referring to the famous Hebrew patriarch and ex-juvenile delinquent, who was found in the bullrushes outside the window in Cairo where I am writing this. My Moses is a much humbler and less disturbing character altogether who gets his manna from much more sordid sources.

I hope you will bear with me while I tell you about Moses, for he is one of the great worthies of Cairo who, in his picturesque and frankly roguish way, represents the real spirit of Egypt much more faithfully than any of the wealthy and well-groomed pashas in Savile Row suits and crimson tarbooshes who sit around with the exotic entourage in Shepheard's Hotel and the Semiramis drinking coffee like treacle and running down England in their polished Oxford accents. There is nothing like that about Moses. He is the real thing. He is dressed very much as his famous namesake was five thousand years ago and he takes no sides in anything. Moses commandeered me the moment I arrived at the Cairo Museum of Antiquities, where they keep the memory of mankind in glass cases. Where he came from is still a mystery, for I'll swear there was nobody there when he suddenly began to address me out of the void.

"This way, my lord," he said, with a gracious bow. "Welcome to our famous museum. We close in an hour, but I will show your lordship and your ladyship not only the treasures of Tutankhamen and Rameses the Great but the whole history of Egypt from pre-historic times down to Cleopatra who threw the whole thing away for her boy-friend." Then he announced, with a hoarse kind of Cockney chuckle, that there is nothing new under the sun and that if we placed ourselves unreservedly in his hands everything, as he put it, "would be fine and dandy."

By this time we were through the turnstiles and Moses had paid for the tickets. It was too late to back out or to tell him our own host was waiting for us upstairs to show us the whole place for nothing at leisure. Moses was master of the situation and he knew it. It was soon clear that Moses was not called that for nothing. All barriers fell down before him. Sleeping sentinels woke up at his approach and dark places sprang into radiance at a mere wave of his wand. All the time he prattled away in a queer but exceedingly entertaining gibberish about scarabs and hawks, vultures and cobras and pointed out to us the royal cartouches and hieratic dances on the sarcophagi of the great Pharaohs and their nobles.

More than anything, however, Moses is obsessed by what he calls "the evil eye" and every now and then when we came across a particularly nasty-looking optic glaring at us from some ancient piece of granite he would make us link hands and repeat some mumbo-jumbo after him to ward off the curse of Amenophis or somebody like that. During the dull moments between corpses he told us he was a Sudanese and was born in Khartoum on the day General Gordon was killed. He is very proud of his English, which he learned at Wembley during the exhibition when he was a guard at the Sudanese Pavilion. My impression was that he is a little offended with Gerald Barry for overlooking him this time.

What happened to our host I cannot say, for I never found him. Moses was too much for me. In the end he charged me a pound, which was four times the proper rate, and tried to convince me he had paid 10*s*. to get us in. But we did not grudge him that, for he was worth every penny of it. As we left him he took me aside and said if I could give her ladyship the slip later on he would show me something of the social background of modern Egypt. He was not offended when I told him to go to blazes. He understood quite well and, giving us a curious cross-fingered salute to "ward off the evil eye," he cried, "Fine and dandy" and dematerialised as mysteriously as he came.

*May 7th*, 1951

# WHO WOULD BE A CAMEL?

LUXOR.

AFTER giving the matter the most careful consideration and looking at it from every conceivable angle I cannot see any point in being a camel. There are certain advantages in being a tortoise or a mosquito, and if the worst comes to the worst and we all come back as animals, as Buddha said, one could, I imagine, get on fairly well as a boa-constrictor, a duck-billed platypus or even a Colorado beetle. But there seems to be no advantage whatever in being a camel. From the day he is born and staggers to his spindly shanks till the day he sinks back into the sand for the last time, worn out with weights and blows, the camel's lot is not a happy one. His life is one endless travail with no rewards but an occasional bellyful of grass and a humpful of brackish water once a month. Even the poor blind mole, burrowing away beneath the Sussex Downs, works only for himself and no doubt enjoys the dark enchantment of his silent subterranean world. The tethered goat, who seems sad enough, has a change of scenery sometimes and nobody—at any rate since Caligula—has thought of harnessing the hippopotamus.

The only creatures which have as miserable a time as the camel—except, of course, all creatures in cages—are the reindeer and the mule, but they have consolations denied to the dromedary. The mule may be miserable but, as someone pointed out, he has no pride of ancestry or hope of posterity, and is therefore not troubled with dynastic problems like the camel, who has to plod along beneath his load with the heirs to his misery padding behind him. And the reindeer, though he has little to eat but frozen grass and nothing to drink but snow, is loved by everybody and has his own frosty corner in fairyland.

There are not even such negative joys for the camel. Even when his master is kind to him his life is one endless vista of scorching sands and brazen skies, interminable roads and intolerable burdens, with clouds of flies buzzing in his eyes and nostrils and stinging scorpions round his rump when he sits down among the hot stones. His one hope, that the last straw will break his back, is an illusion. In Egypt there is nothing so kindly to the camel as a last straw. The camel's tragedy, in fact, is that there are no last straws. It is his heart and not his back that is broken.

Before I came to Egypt the camel was nothing to me but a stupid animal, with one or two humps, who chewed the cud and carried

romantic characters like Rudolph Valentino and Lawrence of Arabia across the desert on their amorous or bellicose adventures. On the rare occasions I had reason for writing about it I probably called it the ship of the desert to fill a whole line. I don't suppose I had ever seen more than two or three camels at a time before I went to Luxor and saw hundreds of them toiling away in the fields, working water mills, grinding corn, ploughing, carrying enormous loads of wood, going round and round yoked blindfold to wheels like Samson "eyeless in Gaza at the mill with slaves," and posing for photographs before the Colossi of Memnon with leggy American girls hanging on to their humps. I must have had a penny ride on the dromedary when I was a boy, and I once saw a string of camels in Drury Lane when "The Desert Song" was on there. It is only when you see camels in the mass moving miserably along under their ponderous loads that you realise the sad existence that they lead.

So far as I know there are no wild camels, and they tell me that the bedouin's camel far out in the desert has a happier time of it than the unhappy commercialised brutes you see swaying along in the dust clouds between the big towns. The trouble about the camel is that he is far too placid. Sometimes he bites, but he seldom turns on his driver, as a mule does occasionally, and kick him over the Pyramids. But Africa is awakening, and the camel may wake up, too. One day, who knows, a Nye Bevan among camels may arise in the caravan. And who can foretell what dust he will kick up in the desert?

*May 3rd,* 1951


## WHERE ST. GEORGE SLEW THE DRAGON

BEIRUT.

WE left Cyprus with great reluctance accompanied by a glittering woman from Milwaukee, whom we had last seen shimmering in the shadows of Tutankhamen's tomb. When we left the hotel in Nicosia the thunder was rumbling in the Kyrenian mountains like Omar Khayyam's drum, and the lightning—as Burns once said quite unscientifically—flashed from pole to pole. And when we got to the airport the hailstones were dancing like marbles on the runway. When we reached Beirut an hour later we stepped out into a heat wave. The asphalt was bubbling like boiling treacle and even the snows of Lebanon high up over the town looked flushed in the waves of shimmering heat. The glittering lady who carried a mink cape said she was "darned" and "doggone" if she had ever known such weather.

It was quite by accident, but most appropriate, that I arrived in Beirut on my birthday. For it was there in what is now called, by an exquisite piece of municipal irony, Slaughterhouse Street, that St. George slew the dragon. Nobody knows why April 23rd was selected as St. George's Day and there is probably as much, or as little, foundation for the date as there is for the event.

From the little that is known of him St. George appears to have been a Cappadocian contractor who sold bacon—the soldiers said it was bad—to the army ; and he no doubt diddled the Government very much as his townsmen do today when they get the chance. It was this bacon deal that led Napoleon to describe England as a nation of shopkeepers—stealing the phrase from his fellow Corsican Paoli, who is buried among the railway tracks at the back of Euston Station.

But whoever picked on April 23rd it was a good day to choose, and I am pleased that I had the good luck to choose it, too, along with Shakespeare, Cervantes, Thomas Hardy, Stafford Cripps, Shirley Temple, Lord Haw Haw, Larry Cade, of *The Star*, Mervyn Herbert, my foreign editor, and Charlie Brooks, of the Manchester Press Club. On behalf of them all I went along to Slaughterhouse Street to pay our respects to our patron saint, only to find that the scene of his exploit is now occupied by the Al-Khodr Mosque. This was a bit of a blow until I found out that Al-Khodr is the Arabic for St. George, so I took my shoes off and went in. The old mosque, which was originally St. George's Church, was built by the Crusaders.

To me, however, there was much more drama and a great deal more poignancy in another April memorial I came across by chance in another church just before I left. This is a small stained glass window in the English Church of All Saints which stands on the sea-front. The little window which is let into the sea wall of the church—it is in the diocese of Jerusalem—is in memory of Alexander Douglas Cruikshank "who died on April 16, 1922, aged one year." That is all it says about wee Alec and nobody could tell me any more. But in its way it is enough. For though he only lived one year in this world he has this little window looking out on St. George's Bay all to himself.

And in the evening when the sun goes down it is lit up by the shining snows of Lebanon and every now and then somebody comes and leaves a bunch of roses or a sprig of jacaranda on the window-sill. Best of all, on each side of little Alec stand Richard Cœur de Lion and St. Louis of France with their lances at rest and their pennants flying. Even St. George up there in Slaughterhouse Street hasn't got company like that !

*May 23rd,* 1951

# PART SIX

# *Epitaph*

## SLEEPLESS, I WRITE MY EPITAPH

LONDON.

THE curse of the Crusader is still upon me. Even now, ten days after my return from Erin's Isle, I can still feel his icy finger on my fevered brow. And here I lie, "a sheer hulk," like poor Tom Bowling, helpless, hot and miserable and almost sunk without trace. Sometimes I feel, as I float drowsily in the aromatic mists of Friar's Balsam Land, like one of those big pink jelly-fish you see in a deep green Cornish cove swaying from sun to shadow all day long, now warm, now cold, but always clammy. And then, when for a moment or two I emerge from the mist, I feel like the unhappy man mentioned by my friend Harold Davies in the Commons the other day who suffered from rheumatoid arthritis and St. Vitus's Dance at the same time, only in my case to make matters merrier still I have what Anna Christie's father would have called "dat ole debbil" duodenum as well.

You can, however, get used to anything in time—which is the main argument against hell—and I have learned how to cough without shattering myself to bits, how to toss and turn without tearing my heart out, and in a day or two I hope to carry on without breathing at all. But the real curse of sickness is the people who won't let you alone. Since I crawled into bed last Saturday week the place has been full of plumbers, plasterers, telephone men, war damage assessors, snow-shovellers, electricians and gas-meter men, and now they tell me there is a man called Winston Churchill on his way to mend the radio.

You may ask what all these men are doing here. Well, I should explain that by an ingenious arrangement of broken windows, shattered skylights and rickety doors there is a permanent hurricane blowing through my flat, which I am told is clean and healthy and keeps the place free from bubonic plague and the tsetse fly. There is a letter somewhere saying that "the men" would soon be round to put things right. But this letter was received in November, 1944, when the flying bombs were playing five-finger exercises on the lake in Regent's Park, to steal an image my beloved master Herbert Sidebotham no longer needs in the Elysian Fields where he is now deep in some academic—and ambrosial—dispute with Cicero and Quintillian.

But worst of all is this business of getting to sleep. The leech has given me some green things packed with deadly poison, but they might just as well be goblets of Veuve Clicquot. They make me bright and fill the night with wild imaginings. I have tried every known soporific.

I go through the company reports in *The Times* only to find them full of rich romance and thrilling tales of Rio Tintos, Antofagastas and Trinidados and wild goings on at Pabbojan, Kuala Lumpur and Vallombrosa. I might as well read Somerset Maugham and be done with it. In the end I gave it up and decided instead to write my own epitaph as many other insomniacs have done before me. And with it I may conclude this woeful wail in case, as Harry Lauder has been saying for so many years, this is positively my last appearance. Here it is for what it's worth:

> When the time comes when I am not
> Some friend no doubt will say "His head was hot."
> While some fair charmer when the tale is told
> Will sigh and murmur "And his feet were cold,"
> And then I hope they'll walk off arm in arm
> And say together "But his heart was warm."

*February 24th*, 1948